Resume, Application, and Letter Tips for People With Hot and Not-So-Hot Backgrounds

By Ron and Caryl Krannich

CAREER AND BUSINESS BOOKS AND SOFTWARE
101 Secrets of Highly Effective Speakers
201 Dynamite Job Search Letters
The $100,000+ Entrepreneur
America's Top 100 Jobs for People Without a Four-Year Degree
America's Top Jobs for People Re-Entering the Workforce
America's Top Internet Job Sites
Best Jobs for the 21st Century
Best Resumes and Letters for Ex-Offenders
Blue Collar Resume and Job Hunting Guide
Change Your Job, Change Your Life
The Complete Guide to Public Employment
The Directory of Federal Jobs and Employers
Discover the Best Jobs for You!
Dynamite Salary Negotiations
Dynamite Tele-Search
The Educator's Guide to Alternative Jobs and Careers
The Ex-Offender's Job Hunting Guide
The Ex-Offender's Quick Job Hunting Guide
Find a Federal Job Fast!
From Air Force Blue to Corporate Gray
From Army Green to Corporate Gray
From Navy Blue to Corporate Gray
Get a Raise in 7 Days
High Impact Resumes and Letters
I Can't Believe They Asked Me That!
I Want to Do Something Else, But I'm Not Sure What It Is
Interview for Success
The Job Hunting Guide: Transitioning From College to Career
Job Hunting Tips for People With Hot and Not-So-Hot Backgrounds
Job Interview Tips for People With Not-So-Hot Backgrounds
Job-Power Source and Ultimate Job Source (software)
Jobs and Careers With Nonprofit Organizations
Military Transition to Civilian Success
Military Resumes and Cover Letters
Nail the Cover Letter!
Nail the Job Interview!
Nail the Resume!
No One Will Hire Me!
Overcoming Barriers to Employment
Re-Careering in Turbulent Times
Savvy Interviewing
The Savvy Networker
The Savvy Resume Writer
Win the Interview, Win the Job

TRAVEL AND INTERNATIONAL BOOKS
Best Resumes and CVs for International Jobs
The Complete Guide to International Jobs and Careers
The Directory of Websites for International Jobs
International Jobs Directory
Jobs for Travel Lovers
Shopping in Exotic Places
Shopping the Exotic South Pacific
Travel Planning On the Internet
Treasures and Pleasures of Australia
Treasures and Pleasures of Bermuda
Treasures and Pleasures of China
Treasures and Pleasures of Egypt
Treasures and Pleasures of Hong Kong
Treasures and Pleasures of India
Treasures and Pleasures of Indonesia
Treasures and Pleasures of Italy
Treasures and Pleasures of Mexico
Treasures and Pleasures of Paris
Treasures and Pleasures of Rio and São Paulo
Treasures and Pleasures of Santa Fe, Taos, and Albuquerque
Treasures and Pleasures of Singapore
Treasures and Pleasures of South America
Treasures and Pleasures of Southern Africa
Treasures and Pleasures of Thailand and Myanmar
Treasures and Pleasures of Turkey
Treasures and Pleasures of Vietnam and Cambodia

Resume, Application, and Letter Tips
for People with Hot and Not-So-Hot Backgrounds

185 Tips for Landing the Perfect Job

Ron and Caryl Krannich, Ph.Ds

IMPACT PUBLICATIONS
Manassas Park, VA

Resume, Application, and Letter Tips for People With Hot and Not-So-Hot Backgrounds

ISBN: 1-57023-240-7

Library of Congress: 2006925550

Publisher: For information on Impact Publications, including current and forthcoming publications, authors, press kits, online bookstore, and submission requirements, visit the left navigation bar on the front page of our main company website: www.impactpublications.com.

Publicity/Rights: For information on publicity, author interviews, and subsidiary rights, contact the Media Relations Department: Tel. 703-361-7300, Fax 703-335-9486, or email: query@impactpublications.com.

Sales/Distribution: All bookstore sales are handled through Impact's trade distributor: National Book Network, 15200 NBN Way, Blue Ridge Summit, PA 17214, Tel. 1-800-462-6420. All special sales and distribution inquiries should be directed to the publisher: Sales Department, IMPACT PUBLICATIONS, 9104 Manassas Drive, Suite N, Manassas Park, VA 20111-5211, Tel. 703-361-7300, Fax 703-335-9486, or email: query@impactpublications.com.

Contents

Index to Tips

Job Search Tips for Success

Resume Strategies, Issues, and Organization

Writing Your Own Resume With Impact

Designing, Producing, and Evaluating Your Resume

Marketing, Distributing, and Following Up Your Resume

Completing Effective Applications

Effective Cover and Job Search Letters

1

Making Smart Decisions the Rest of Your Worklife

EACH YEAR OVER 25 MILLION Americans conduct some form of job search involving the writing, production, and distribution of resumes, letters, and applications. While all of these anxious job seekers will eventually find a job, some will do so more efficiently and effectively because of the quality of their writing and marketing activities. Indeed, many of them avoid common errors associated with writing their way to job search success. They only send a few resumes and letters or complete a couple of applications to quickly land job interviews that result in attractive job offers. Rather than spend the customary three to six months looking for a job, they connect with the right employer within a few days or weeks.

Meet Proactive Job Seekers

What do these successful job seekers know and do that is different from their less successful counterparts? While some of them may get lucky – be in the right place at the right time – most understand the importance of good communication and relationships and accordingly take actions that produce positive outcomes. Focusing on making smart decisions, these proactive job seekers make career moves with relative ease.

Finding a job is not rocket science. It involves a well-defined process that can be learned and routinized. Above all, it requires new knowledge and skills and some basic attitudinal and behavioral changes that are

1

specified in the many tips and techniques outlined in this book. Once you acquire the requisite knowledge, skills, attitudes, and behaviors, you will be well prepared to make important job and career changes the rest of your life.

Developing a New Mindset

This book is all about bringing greater clarity to an important subject that can change your life – connecting to the right job, one you really do well and enjoy doing. Whether you have a hot or not-so-hot background really doesn't matter since the final outcome is the same – landing a great job. Not just any job, but one you really love. Accomplishing this goal requires that you initially approach this subject with an open mind, positive attitude, motivation, drive, purpose, persistence, and a willingness to learn. It means challenging some of your own beliefs about how to best approach the job market and acquiring new writing skills for clearly communicating your qualifications to prospective employers.

> *No one is responsible for giving you a job or keeping you on a job indefinitely.*

Finding good jobs and enjoying a productive career are all about making smart decisions and taking responsibility for your own employment fate. After all, no one is responsible for giving you a job or keeping you on a job indefinitely. At the very least, you must be entrepreneurial in securing your future. You must change your thinking **before** you can change your behavior and your life.

Choose to Be a Winner

Much of success in life is all about taking personal responsibility for your choices as well as making smart choices. While some people lack opportunities because of fundamental choices or circumstances beyond their control – choose to live in a community with few well-paying jobs or experience chronic or debilitating illnesses that prevent them from holding a normal job – most people have the power to make choices that can improve their employability, income, and relationships. They regularly make decisions about their education and training, spending patterns, eating and drinking habits, and personal relationships. All of these decisions have consequences.

But the outcomes of individual choices are very different. Some people live extremely dysfunctional lives whereas others seem to be successful at everything they do. Many people regularly spend more money than they make, live from paycheck to paycheck, incur debilitating credit card debts, work in dead-end jobs, lack attractive workplace habits, frequently lose their jobs, neglect their families, experience failed relationships, engage in unhealthy behaviors, express anger publicly, become violent, or have run-ins with the criminal justice system. Such individuals soon become "risky business" for employers, who prefer hiring people they can trust to work in the best interests of the company.

Habits – both good and bad – form early in life and are difficult to change. Successful people often engage in risky behaviors that repeatedly result in positive outcomes. On the other hand, dysfunctional individuals, who often exhibit co-occurring disorders or multiple negative behaviors (substance abuse, anger, depression), frequently make decisions that have disastrous outcomes in several areas

> *Successful people often engage in risky behaviors that result in positive outcomes.*

of their lives – from employment and consumption to family relations and public behavior. Accumulating numerous red flags that define their not-so-hot backgrounds, many of these people simply don't understand how, nor are they sufficiently motivated, to make good decisions that result in positive outcomes for themselves and others around them. These losers make a habit of failure rather than a habit of success. Only major cognitive therapy that focuses on changing individual decision-making seems to have a positive impact on such individuals. If you run with dysfunctional people, you, too, may become a loser in the game of life.

What do successful job seekers do that separates them from their less successful counterparts? What critical choices do they make? How do they approach their job search, communicate with potential employers, complete applications, market their resumes and letters, and follow through to get job interviews? Are there some simple tips and techniques you can acquire from them that will enhance your own job search communication and employability? What can we learn from such successful job seekers?

You Are What You Write

It's no secret that you are what you write in the eyes of employers who know little or nothing about you. After all, you are a stranger who is trying to open the doors of individuals and companies that may be skeptical of your background and motivations. In fact, every day employers make numerous hiring mistakes. Unfortunately, they should have recognized potential red flags early on in the screening and hiring processes, especially when they read and reviewed the candidate's resume, letter, and/or application. Overlooking important clues to potential problems, they make costly hiring errors they could have easily avoided had they initially "read between the lines."

> *Whatever first impression you make will most likely be in writing – your resume, letter, application, or written response to an e-mail.*

Your first encounter with a prospective employer is often over the Internet via e-mail and/or by completing an online form or through the mail in the form of a paper resume, letter, or application. Whether on paper or in an electronic medium, what you say and how you communicate it about yourself and your future performance can make a significant difference between being accepted or rejected for a job interview – the critical first step to getting a job offer.

Making First Electronic and Paper Impressions

Given the increased digitalization of communication, chances are much of your job search writing will take place over the Internet rather than through the mail. In fact, whatever first impression you make on a prospective employer will likely be in **writing** – your resume, letter, application, or written response to an e-mail. Looking for competence in your "tea leaves," many employers will ask you to complete an online profile, which is essentially a mini resume or application, e-mail your resume, or respond to their e-mailed questions **prior to** meeting you by voice over the telephone or in a face-to-face interview. These are important screening mediums that primarily rely on the written word. While the medium may be different, the message is basically the same – you are trying to communicate your qualifications to prospective employers. Accordingly, recipients who receive electronic communications are just as unforgiving of writing errors as recipients of paper communication.

Whatever medium you choose – electronic or paper – it's critically important that your written communication be **perfect**. Unfortunately, the Internet and e-mail have become quick, easy, and raw forms of communication where individuals exhibit all types of bad writing habits, especially spelling, grammar, and punctuation errors, that speak loudly about candidates' character, competence, and future performance.

But employers are less tolerant of writing mistakes from candidates. Individuals who are otherwise relatively literate and competent often project just the opposite image when writing to strangers, because they fail to carefully craft their online communications. Since your job may require quick online written communication (you may not have the luxury to ponder, edit, and re-write your messages), how well you perform in writing during your job search is a strong indicator of how you will perform in similar tasks on the job.

If you were an employer, how seriously would you take someone who wrote to you with spelling, punctuation, and grammatical errors? Would you want to hire them for a job that involves communicating with others about your company, products, and services? What kind of image would they present of you to others who are looking for competence in your operations?

Writing at any stage of your job search is serious business. Keep in mind that what and how you write to a prospective employer may be an initial test of your future competence with the employer. Indeed, a single writing error can immediately raise a red flag that could knock you out of the competition.

Since you are a **stranger** to most employers, who know nothing about you and your accomplishments, your job is to convince them to take some time to seriously consider your candidacy. You want them to invite you to a job interview based on your writing skills. Here's one of the most important guiding principles for directing your job search activities:

You must effectively communicate your value to employers in writing prior to meeting them in person for the critical job interview.

Written Communications for Everyone

The old application distinctions between blue collar and white collar workers are gradually breaking down when we look at how employers screen candidates today. Blue collar workers used to primarily complete application forms in order to get interviews. Resumes and letters were primarily seen as application mediums for white collar workers.

With the increased use of the Internet, scanning technology, and electronic screening devices in the recruitment and hiring process, both blue collar and white collar workers need to know how to best write resumes and letters and complete applications. Blue collar workers are increasingly advised to complete a resume prior to applying for jobs (see our *Blue Collar Resume and Job Hunting Guide*). Many white collar workers are required to complete **online profiles**, which are essentially a combination mini resume and application form, prior to being invited to an interview.

Therefore, it's very important that all job seekers learn how to best communicate their qualifications to potential employers through resumes, applications, and letters. After all, most employers want to see you on paper, or on a computer screen, prior to meeting you in person. Resumes, applications, and letters serve as important devices for screening candidates for job interviews. Here's the bottom line for today's job seeker: without a well-crafted resume, application, or letter, your chances for getting a job interview will be greatly diminished.

Tips to Enhance Your Employability

The purpose of this book is to improve your employability through written communication. Since most job seekers will make their initial contact with an employer through the written word, it's extremely important that you make the very best impression through what and how you write. It's only after you have been invited to an interview that you need to focus on your interpersonal verbal and nonverbal skills involving small talk and answering and asking questions. In the meantime, you need to put together the perfect written package that will grab the attention of potential employers who, in turn, will be curious enough to invite you to a job interview in order to learn more about your suitability for employment with their organization.

So how do you do this? Let's start by taking a look at how you plan to organize your job search. What critical decisions will you make at this stage of your job search? As you will see in the following pages, many of our resume, application, and letter tips are directly related to our preliminary advice in Chapter 2 on how to best organize your job search for maximum impact on prospective employers.

2

Job Search Tips for Success

E VERY DAY HUNDREDS OF employers collect, as well as joke about, stories of candidates who made job search errors. While most such errors relate to resume, application, and letter problems, many others focus on the job interview, such as arriving late for the interview, bringing a child to an interview, smelling like a perfume factory, dressing inappropriately, confessing negatives, asking about salary and benefits early in the interview, begging for the job, and quitting a job before being offered a new position (an invitation to a job interview is not a job offer!). Compilation of these errors can easily be the subject of a separate book devoted to "sins and errors of ineffective job seekers!"

But the most common job search error is the failure to organize one's job search as a step-by-step process and then following through with determination and persistence. As you will see in the rest of this chapter, this single error will affect all other steps in the job search process.

TIP #1
Test your job search I.Q.

Let's begin by examining how well prepared you are to organize and implement an effective job search. There are no right or wrong answers to the following quiz. Most of the issues included here will be addressed in

8

each of the 10 steps. Collectively designed to measure your job search competence, this exercise will give you useful feedback by indicating your current level of job search information, skills, and strategies as well as identifying those you need to develop and improve. Identify your level of job search competence by completing the following exercise:

INSTRUCTIONS: Respond to each statement by circling which number at the right best represents your situation.

SCALE: 1 = Strongly agree   4 = Disagree
              2 = Agree   5 = Strongly disagree
              3 = Maybe, not certain

1. I know what motivates me to excel at work.   1   2   3   4   5

2. I can identify my strongest abilities and skills.   1   2   3   4   5

3. I have seven major achievements that reveal
   a pattern of interests and abilities that are
   relevant to my job and career.   1   2   3   4   5

4. I know what I both like and dislike in work.   1   2   3   4   5

5. I know what I want to do during the next
   10 years.   1   2   3   4   5

6. I have a well defined career objective that
   directs my job search toward certain
   organizations and employers.   1   2   3   4   5

7. I know what skills I can offer employers in
   different occupations.   1   2   3   4   5

8. I know what skills employers most seek in
   candidates.   1   2   3   4   5

9. I can clearly explain to employers what I do
   well and enjoy doing.   1   2   3   4   5

10. I can specify why employers should hire me.   1   2   3   4   5

11. I can gain the support of family and friends
    for making a job or career change.   1   2   3   4   5

12. I can find 10 to 20 hours a week to conduct
    a job search.   1   2   3   4   5

13. I have the financial ability to sustain a
    three-month job search.   1   2   3   4   5

14. I can conduct library and Internet research
    on different occupations, employers,
    organizations, and communities.   1   2   3   4   5

15. I can write different types of effective resumes
    and job search/thank you letters.   1   2   3   4   5

16. I can produce and distribute resumes and
    letters to the right people.   1   2   3   4   5

17. I can list my major accomplishments.   1   2   3   4   5

18. I can identify and target employers I want
    to interview.   1   2   3   4   5

19. I know how to use the Internet to conduct
    employment research and network.   1   2   3   4   5

20. I know which websites are best for posting
    my resumes and browsing job postings.   1   2   3   4   5

21. I know how much time I should spend
    conducting an online job search.   1   2   3   4   5

22. I can develop a job referral network.   1   2   3   4   5

23. I can persuade others to join in forming
    a job search support group.   1   2   3   4   5

24. I can look for job leads.   1   2   3   4   5

25. I can use the telephone to develop prospects
    and get referrals and interviews.   1   2   3   4   5

26. I can plan and implement an effective
    direct-mail job search campaign.   1   2   3   4   5

27. I can persuade employers to interview me.   1   2   3   4   5

28 I have a list of at least 10 questions about the
    company I need to ask during interviews.   1   2   3   4   5

29. I know the best time to talk about salary with
    an employer.   1   2   3   4   5

30. I know what I want to do with my life over the next 10 years.	1 2 3 4 5	
31. I have a clear pattern of accomplishments which I can explain to employers, giving examples.	1 2 3 4 5	
32. I have little difficulty in making cold calls and striking up conversations with strangers.	1 2 3 4 5	
33. I usually take responsibility for my own actions rather than blame other people for my situation or circumstance.	1 2 3 4 5	
34. I can generate at least one job interview for every 10 job search contacts I make.	1 2 3 4 5	
35. I can follow up on job interviews.	1 2 3 4 5	
36. I can negotiate a salary 10-20% above what an employer initially offers.	1 2 3 4 5	
37. I can persuade an employer to renegotiate my salary after six months on the job.	1 2 3 4 5	
38. I can create a position for myself in an organization.	1 2 3 4 5	

TOTAL

Calculate your potential job search effectiveness by adding the numbers you circled for an overall score. If your total is more than 90 points, you need to work on developing your job search. How you scored each item will indicate to what degree you need to work on improving specific job search skills. If your score is under 60 points, you are well on your way toward job search success!

TIP #2
Organize your job search as a 10-step sequential process.

The diagram on page 12 illustrates the 10 steps to job search success. Each step needs to be completed in the order outlined in this diagram.

10 Steps to Job Search Success

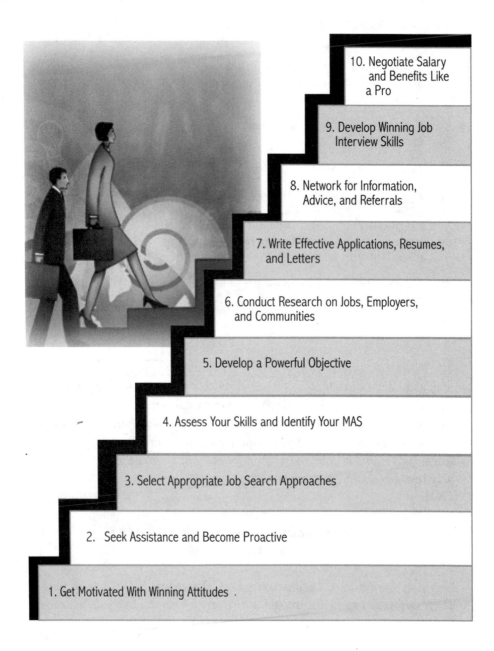

10. Negotiate Salary and Benefits Like a Pro

9. Develop Winning Job Interview Skills

8. Network for Information, Advice, and Referrals

7. Write Effective Applications, Resumes, and Letters

6. Conduct Research on Jobs, Employers, and Communities

5. Develop a Powerful Objective

4. Assess Your Skills and Identify Your MAS

3. Select Appropriate Job Search Approaches

2. Seek Assistance and Become Proactive

1. Get Motivated With Winning Attitudes

Unfortunately, many job seekers fail to understand each of these steps and how they relate to one another. They often tend to start their job search with Step 7 – write resumes and letters – before knowing what they want to do (Step 5) or knowing what they do well and enjoy doing (Step 4). As a result, they tend to write awful resumes and letters that present a very weak picture of what they have done, can do, and will do in the future. In addition, their job search lacks a sense of purpose and direction. Such job seekers also tend to encounter numerous rejections because they simply don't know how to conduct an effective job search involving all of the 10 steps in their proper order.

Take, for example, Step 1, "Examine and Change Your Attitudes." This establishes the foundation for the remaining nine steps. Without the proper attitudes, which also affect your motivation and point you in the right direction, you will have difficulty completing the other steps. Step 4, "Assess Your Skills and Identify Your MAS," is one of the most important steps for completing Steps 5 through 10.

We strongly recommend that you frequently refer to the diagram on page 12 throughout your job search. Be sure to take the time to complete each step thoroughly and in the proper order. If you do this, you will be well on your way to finding a job that is right for you. We provide details on the major job search steps in *Change Your Job, Change Your Life* (Impact Publications).

TIP #3
Focus on implementation by developing
a time line for achieving success.

Job search success is all about **implementation** – the ability to transform a plan into action that produces desired outcomes. Anyone can find a job, but finding a really good job that you do well and enjoy doing will involve a major investment of your time. If you are a busy person who feels you have little spare time for anything, you simply **must** find time to conduct your job search. If you don't think you can find sufficient time to do this right, consider this fact of employment life:

> **Your new job could be worth an additional $1 million in income over the next several years, especially if you land a job that pays substantially more than your past or current job.**

So just how much is your time worth? $5, $10, $25, $50, or $100 an hour? If every hour you invest in your job search results in $100 of additional income, you may decide you can indeed find enough time to conduct a serious job search. Start by analyzing how you currently use your time. Most people, for example, spend 80 percent of their time on trivia and 20 percent on things that really matter. You need to reverse those percentages so that 80 percent of your time is used effectively. You can start reorganizing your time by addressing a few basic time management questions:

- Do you know how to say "no" or do you tend to say "yes" to everything?

- Do you place a dollar value on your time and act accordingly?

- Do you let others control your time or do you take charge of your time?

- Do you quickly dispense with your junk mail or do your ponder and save it?

- Do you set priorities, use a scheduling calendar, and set work targets?

> *Most job seekers take from three to six months to find a job in today's job market.*

Chances are you can find time for your job search if you first reassess how you currently time use. Finding a job can take as little as a few days or as much as several months, depending on the level of job and how you organize your job search. Most job seekers take from three to six months to find a job in today's job market. As indicated in the hypothetical organizational chart on page 15, implementing the job search steps outlined in the figure on page 12 may take place over a six-month period. Depending on a combination of good planning, serendipity, and luck, job interviews and offers can occur at any time. You can accelerate this time line by spending more time on your job search. If, for example, you only devote 10 hours

Organization of Job Search Activities

Activity	Weeks
	1 2 3 4 5 6 7 8 9 10 11 12 13 14 15 16 17 18 19 20 21 22 23 24
▪ Thinking, questioning, listening, evaluating, adjusting	▮ (weeks 1–24)
▪ Identifying abilities and skills	▮ (weeks 3–4)
▪ Setting objectives	▮ (weeks 4–5)
▪ Writing resume	▮ (weeks 5–6)
▪ Conducting research	▮ (weeks 1–24)
▪ Prospecting, referrals, networking	▮ (weeks 1–24)
▪ Interviewing	┆ (weeks 9–24, intermittent)
▪ Receiving and negotiating job offers	┆ (weeks 13–24, intermittent)

a week to finding a job, chances are it may take you a long time to connect with the right job. However, if you make this a full-time endeavor by spending 40 to 80 hours a week engaged in various job search activities, you may be able to shorten your job search time from three months to one month. Your success in finding a job will depend on how much time and effort you devote to your search. Whatever you do, don't get discouraged and give up prematurely after encountering a few rejections (see Tip #18). Keeping focused on completing and repeating each job search activity over a 24-week time line will eventually pay off with a job that's right for you.

TIP #4
Commit yourself in writing to achieving concrete results.

You must keep focused, motivated, and committed throughout your job search. It's not surprising that the single most important impediment to conducting a successful job search is the **failure to implement**. While you can have all the dreams, plans, and positive thinking you want, if you don't translate those dreams, plans, and thinking into daily and weekly plans of action, you will be going nowhere with your job search. Based on your self-assessment activities (Step 4), you need to specify how your objective (Step 5) will translate into research, resume and letter writing, and networking activities (Steps 6-8). One of the best ways to do this is to commit yourself in writing by completing the Job Search Contract and Weekly Job Performance and Planning Report on pages 17 and 18. This contract and report will serve as key documents for both prioritizing and implementing your job search as well as keeping you focused and motivated on what you need to do in order to conduct a successful job search.

TIP #5
Make your attitude central to everything you do in your job search.

Whether you are aware of it or not, your attitude will be a powerful determiner of your job search success. In fact, your attitude might drag you down a road to failure. Attitude is the very first job search step we identified in the figure on page 12. It's the basis for everything that fol-

Job Search Contract

1. I'm committed to changing my life by changing my job. Today's date is _____.

2. I will manage my time so that I can successfully complete my job search and find a high quality job. I will begin changing my time management behavior on _____.

3. I will begin my job search on _____.

4. I will involve _____ with my job search.
   (individual/group)

5. I will spend at least one week conducting library research on different jobs, employers, and organizations. I will begin this research during the week of _____.

6. I will complete my skills identification step by _____.

7. I will complete my objective statement by _____.

8. I will complete my resume by _____.

9. Each week I will:

   ■ make _____ new job contacts.

   ■ conduct _____ informational interviews.

   ■ follow up on _____ referrals.

10. My first job interview will take place during the week of _____.

11. I will begin my new job by _____.

12. I will make a habit of learning one new skill each year.

Signature: _____

Date: _____

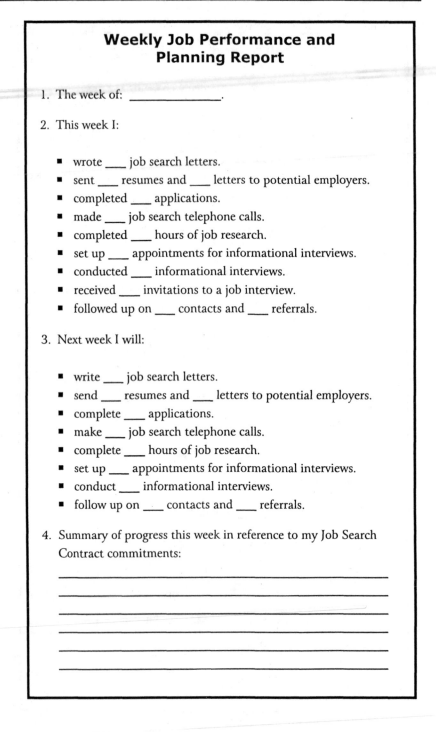

Weekly Job Performance and Planning Report

1. The week of: _____.

2. This week I:

   - wrote ____ job search letters.
   - sent ____ resumes and ____ letters to potential employers.
   - completed ____ applications.
   - made ____ job search telephone calls.
   - completed ____ hours of job research.
   - set up ____ appointments for informational interviews.
   - conducted ____ informational interviews.
   - received ____ invitations to a job interview.
   - followed up on ____ contacts and ____ referrals.

3. Next week I will:

   - write ____ job search letters.
   - send ____ resumes and ____ letters to potential employers.
   - complete ____ applications.
   - make ____ job search telephone calls.
   - complete ____ hours of job research.
   - set up ____ appointments for informational interviews.
   - conduct ____ informational interviews.
   - follow up on ____ contacts and ____ referrals.

4. Summary of progress this week in reference to my Job Search Contract commitments:

   _____
   _____
   _____
   _____
   _____
   _____

lows. Take a moment to examine your attitude. Is it negative much of the time? Do you often make excuses? Does your attitude show in what you say and do? Are others attracted to you in a positive manner? What motivates you to succeed?

One of the first things you need to do is check the state of your attitude. You can do this by completing the following exercise. Check whether or not you primarily agree ("Yes") or disagree ("No") with each of these statements:

	Yes	**No**
1. Other people often make my work and life difficult.	❏	❏
2. When I get into trouble, it's often because of what someone else did rather than my fault.	❏	❏
3. People often take advantage of me.	❏	❏
4. People less qualified than me often get promoted.	❏	❏
5. I avoid taking risks because I'm afraid of failing.	❏	❏
6. I don't trust many people.	❏	❏
7. Not many people trust me.	❏	❏
8. Not many people I know take responsibility.	❏	❏
9. Most people get ahead because of connections, schmoozing, and politics.	❏	❏
10. In my workplace I am often assigned more duties than other people in similar positions.	❏	❏
11. I expect to be discriminated against in my job search and on the job.	❏	❏
12. I don't feel like I can change many things; I've been dealt this hand, so I'll have to live with it.	❏	❏
13. I've had my share of bad luck.	❏	❏
14. I usually have to do things myself rather than rely on others to get things done.	❏	❏
15. People often pick on me.	❏	❏

16. Employers try to take advantage of job seekers by offering them low salaries.   ❏ ❏

17. I don't like many of the people I have worked with.   ❏ ❏

18. There's not much I can do to get ahead.   ❏ ❏

19. My ideas are not really taken seriously.   ❏ ❏

20. I often think of reasons why other people's ideas won't work.   ❏ ❏

21. Other people are often wrong, but I have to put up with them nonetheless.   ❏ ❏

22. I sometimes respond to suggestions by saying, *"Yes, but . . . ," "I'm not sure . . . ," "I don't think it will work . . . ," "Let's not do that . . ."*   ❏ ❏

23. I don't see why I need to get more education and training.   ❏ ❏

24. I often wish other people would just disappear.   ❏ ❏

25. I sometimes feel depressed.   ❏ ❏

26. I have a hard time getting and staying motivated.   ❏ ❏

27. I don't look forward to going to work.   ❏ ❏

28. Friday is my favorite workday.   ❏ ❏

29. I sometimes come to work late or leave early.   ❏ ❏

30. The jobs I've had haven't reflected my true talents.   ❏ ❏

31. I should have advanced a lot further than where I am today.   ❏ ❏

32. I'm worth a lot more than most employers are willing to pay.   ❏ ❏

33. I've been known to do things behind my boss's back that could get me into trouble.   ❏ ❏

TOTALS   ___ ___

Not all of these statements necessarily reflect bad attitudes or negative behaviors. Some may accurately reflect realities you encounter. In fact, some organizations breed negative attitudes and behaviors among their employees. However, if you checked "Yes" to more than six of these statements, you may be harboring some negative attitudes that affect both your job search and your on-the-job performance. You may want to examine these attitudes as possible **barriers to getting ahead** in your job search as well as on the job. Indeed, you may want to change those attitudes that may be preventing you from making good choices and getting ahead.

TIP #6
Avoid making excuses for your behavior.

Many negative attitudes are related to excuses we make for our behavior. Take, for example, the following list of "100 Excuses for Choosing Poor Behavior" compiled by Rory Donaldson on www.brainsarefun.com. While many of these excuses apply to the child within us – and especially schoolchildren – many also relate to everyone else. He prefaces this list with Rudyard Kipling's observation that *"We have forty million reasons for failure, but not a single excuse"*:

1. It's your fault.
2. I'm not happy.
3. It's too hot.
4. I'm too busy.
5. I'm sad.
6. I didn't sleep well.
7. It's not fair.
8. I wanted to watch TV.
9. I didn't write it down.
10. It's too hard.
11. It's too far away.
12. The teacher didn't explain it.
13. I forgot.
14. The dog was sick.
15. There was too much traffic.
16. I tried.
17. My pencil broke.
18. My grandmother wouldn't let me.
19. You're mean.
20. I didn't know it was today.
21. I'm too tired.
22. My brother was sick.
23. The car broke down.
24. It was snowing.
25. I hurt my foot.
26. I thought it was due tomorrow.
27. The ice was too thin.
28. I ran out of time.
29. I hurt my finger.
30. I don't feel well.
31. You didn't tell me.
32. It was cold.
33. I'm not good at that.
34. I left it in my pocket.
35. He made a face at me.
36. I wasn't.

37. I was rushed.
38. You didn't give it to me.
39. We did that last year.
40. That's not the way we learned at school.
41. His mother said it was O.K.
42. I already did it.
43. It was right here.
44. It's too much work.
45. It stinks.
46. I didn't know it was sharp.
47. I was scared.
48. I was frustrated.
49. I did already.
50. It wasn't in the dictionary.
51. I lost it.
52. Nobody likes me.
53. I have poor self esteem.
54. I'm too happy.
55. I'm sleepy.
56. He hit me.
57. I already know that.
58. I left it at school.
59. It's too easy.
60. It's not important.
61. I couldn't get into my locker.
62. I dropped it.
63. I have a learning disorder.
64. I lost my pencil.
65. My pen leaked.
66. I have an excuse.
67. It got wet.
68. It got dirty.
69. My dog threw up.
70. I missed the bus.
71. I have a different learning style.
72. It was raining.
73. My grandfather was visiting.
74. I didn't know.
75. No one told me.
76. I don't have to.
77. My neck hurts.
78. I ran out of paper.
79. The electricity went out.
80. I don't know how.
81. I can't.
82. I don't know where it is.
83. He hit me first.
84. It's the weekend.
85. I ran out of money.
86. I'm too stupid.
87. My teacher said to do it this way.
88. I watched it at my friend's house.
89. I just cleaned it.
90. My friend got one.
91. You lost it.
92. It takes too much time.
93. He told me I didn't have to.
94. I'm hungry.
95. I couldn't open the door.
96. I'm too important.
97. It spilled.
98. I ran out of batteries.
99. I'm doing something else.
100. I didn't know it was hot.

We and other employers have often encountered 20 additional excuses related to the workplace. Some are even used by candidates during a job interview to explain their on-the-job behavior! Most of these excuses reflect an attitude lacking in responsibility and initiative:

1. No one told me.
2. I did what you said.
3. Your directions were bad.
4. It's not my fault.
5. She did it.
6. It just seemed to happen.
7. It happens a lot.
8. What did he say?

9.	I had a headache.	15.	I thought I wrote it down.
10.	I don't understand why.	16.	That's not my style.
11.	I don't know how to do it.	17.	He told me to do it that way.
12.	That's your problem.	18.	I've got to go now.
13.	It wasn't very good.	19.	Where do you think it went?
14.	Maybe you did it.	20.	We can talk about it later.

When you state such excuses, you literally express attitudes that are not appreciated by employers. People with positive attitudes and proactive behavior do not engage in behaviors that reflect such excuses. They have a "can do" attitude that helps focus their minds on doing those things that are most important to achieving their goals. For example, rather than show up 10 minutes late for a job interview and say they got lost or had bad directions, people with positive attitudes and proactive behavior check out the interview location the day before in anticipation of arriving 10 minutes early. They make no excuses because they plan ahead and engage in no-excuses behavior!

> *People with positive attitudes and proactive behavior have a "can do" attitude that helps focus their minds on achieving results.*

TIP #7
Express positive attitudes desired by employers.

The job search is all about making good first impressions on strangers who know little about your background and capabilities. Whether completing an application, writing a resume, or interviewing for a job, your attitude will show in many different ways, both verbally and nonverbally.

Many job seekers show attitudes of disrespect, deceit, greed, laziness, irresponsibility, carelessness, and calculation – all red flags that will quickly eliminate you from consideration. While some of these attitudes can be spotted on resumes and applications as well as in letters, most of these attitudes are communicated over the telephone or during the critical job interview when employers have a chance to read both verbal and nonverbal behavioral cues. Here are some common mistakes job seekers make that reveal some killer attitudes that also reflect on their character:

Mistake	Attitude/Character
■ Lacks a job objective	Confused and unfocused
■ Misspells words on application, resume, and letters	Careless and uneducated
■ Uses poor grammar	Uneducated
■ Sends resume to the wrong person	Careless and error-prone
■ Arrives late for the job interview	Unreliable and inconsiderate
■ Dresses inappropriately	Unperceptive/insensitive
■ Knows little about the company	Lazy and uninterested
■ Talks about salary and benefits	Greedy and self-centered
■ Bad-mouths previous employer	Disrespectful and angry
■ Doesn't admit to any weaknesses	Disingenuous/calculating
■ Boasts about self	Obnoxious and self-centered
■ Lies about background	Deceitful
■ Lacks eye contact	Shifty and dishonest
■ Blames others for problems	Irresponsible
■ Interrupts and argues	Inconsiderate and impatient
■ Has trouble answering questions	Unprepared and nervous
■ Fails to ask any questions	Uninterested in job
■ Jumps from one extreme to another	Manic and unfocused
■ Fails to follow up the interview	Doesn't care about the job

On the other hand, employers look for attitudes that indicate a candidate has some of the following positive characteristics:

- Accurate
- Adaptable
- Careful
- Competent
- Considerate
- Cooperative
- Dependable
- Determined
- Diligent
- Discreet
- Educated
- Efficient
- Empathic
- Energetic
- Enthusiastic
- Fair
- Focused
- Good-natured
- Happy
- Helpful
- Honest
- Intelligent
- Loyal
- Nice
- Open-minded
- Patient
- Perceptive
- Precise
- Predictable
- Prompt
- Purposeful
- Reliable
- Resourceful
- Respectful

- Responsible
- Self-motivated
- Sensitive
- Sincere
- Skilled
- Tactful

- Team player
- Tenacious
- Tolerant
- Trustworthy
- Warm

TIP #8
Change attitudes that may work against your best interests.

If you have negative attitudes and often need to make excuses for your behavior, you are probably an unhappy person. It's time you took control of both your attitudes and behaviors. Start by identifying several of your negative attitudes and try to transform them into positive attitudes. As you do this, you will begin to identify the positive-minded person you want to be. For starters, examine these sets of negative and positive attitudes that can arise at various stages of the job search, especially during the critical job interview:

Negative Attitude	Positive Attitude
I didn't like my last employer.	It was time for me to move on to a more progressive company.
I haven't been able to find a job in over three months. I really want this one.	I've been learning a great deal during the past several weeks of my job search.
My last two jobs were problems.	I learned a great deal about what I really love to do from those last two jobs.
Do you have a job for me?	I'm in the process of conducting a job search. Do you know anyone who might have an interest in someone with my qualifications?
I can't come in for an interview tomorrow since I'm interviewing for another job. What about Wednesday? That looks good.	I have a conflict tomorrow. Wednesday would be good. Could we do something in the morning?

Yes, I flunked out of college in my sophomore year.	After two years in college I decided to pursue a career in computer sales.
I really hated studying math.	Does this job require math?
Sorry about that spelling error on my resume. I was never good at spelling.	(Doesn't point it out; if the interviewer asked, replied *"It's one that got away."*)
I don't enjoy working in teams.	I work best when given an assignment that allows me to work on my own.
What does this job pay?	How does the pay scale here compare with other firms in the area?
Will I have to work weekends?	What are the normal hours for someone in this position?
I'm three months pregnant. Will your health care program cover my delivery?	Could you tell me more about your benefits, such as health and dental care?
I have to see my therapist once a month. Can I have that day off?	I have an appointment I need to keep the last Friday of each month. Would it be okay if I took off three hours that day?
I've just got out of prison and need a job.	While incarcerated, I turned my life around by getting my GED, learning new skills, and controlling my anger. I'm really excited about becoming a landscape architect and working with your company.

Can you think of any particular negative attitudes you might have that you can restate in positive language? Identify five that relate to your job search and work. State them in both the negative and positive. Respond to these common job interview queries with positive answers:

- Tell me about yourself.
- Why did you leave your last two jobs?
- Why should I hire you?

TIP #9
Approach your job search for positive rather than negative reasons.

A positive attitude, optimism, and enthusiasm are very important when looking for a job. They will help you handle the many psychological ups and downs you are likely to encounter when looking for a job.

If you lost your job or seek a new job because you are unhappy with your current job, chances are you may be approaching your job search for negative reasons. Perhaps you may feel unjustly fired or you dislike your boss or co-workers. Such feelings can be translated into negative attitudes that get communicated to prospective employers. Always keep in mind that employers want to hire positive, energetic, and enthusiastic individuals who also are likely to be intelligent and show initiative. They don't want to hire negative people or those who have an attitude problem or seem to dislike their work. If you have negative reasons for seeking a job, you probably need to improve your attitude. Start by listing five reasons why you are looking for a job:

1. _____

2. _____

3. _____

4. _____

5. _____

Review your list and cross out any negative reasons for seeking a new job. Replace the negative statements with a restatement of the negative reason in a positive way, or with additional positive reasons. Now, rank order all five statements with "1" representing the most important positive reason for seeking a new job.

You also should examine your language when talking about your past, present, and future employment. Everything you include on your resume and in your job search letters should be employer-centered and emphasize the positive, starting with your objective. During job interviews, avoid using words and phrases that might indicate possible negative attitudes or questionable motivations. Common negatives such as *"didn't,"* *"wouldn't,"* *"can't,"* and *"don't"* often communicate the wrong messages to employers:

Negative	Positive
I *didn't* get a raise.	I expected my performance would be better rewarded.
I *wouldn't* take that assignment in Buffalo.	I love this community and want to stay here for many years.
I *can't* afford a car right now.	Transportation should be no problem.
I *don't* know how to operate that program.	I would love to learn how to operate that program.

If asked why you left your previous job, don't talk about negative experiences, disappointments, or history, such as the fact that you didn't like your boss, the people you worked for were basically incompetent, you were passed over for a promotion, you were fired, or you just didn't like working for jerks. While these may be legitimate reasons for leaving and you are being frank and honest, such negative reasons communicate the wrong messages and attitudes to prospective employers, who are interested in hiring your future rather than inheriting your past. Bad-mouthing an employer will raise a red flag about your attitude and behavior, especially since your prospective employer will assume you will probably bad-mouth him or her after you get the job! Instead, focus on the positive and the future by talking about your past accomplishments and your interest in seeking new opportunities and more fully utilizing your skills.

Your positive attitude may become your most important asset throughout your job search.

If you keep a positive attitude and focus on the positive – what's right about you, the job, and the employer – you'll quickly discover this positive approach will be contagious. It will help motivate you, keep your morale up despite rejections, and communicate optimism and enthusiasm to those around you. Indeed, your positive attitude may become your most important asset throughout your job search.

TIP #10
Don't spend a great deal of time looking for jobs
in newspapers or on the Internet.

Most job seekers spend a great deal of time looking for and responding to job vacancies in the classified section of newspapers and on employment websites. They send resumes and letters in response to such listings in the hope of being called for a job interview. Such activities give job seekers a false sense of making progress in the job market, because they believe they are doing something they think will result in a job. These also are the main job search activities of many frustrated job seekers who complain there no jobs available for them or that employers are not interested in hiring them. We hear this complaint again and again from job seekers who are primarily focused on finding employment through newspapers and the Internet. But the likelihood of landing a job this way is similar to being struck by lightning – very unlikely. In fact, these are the least effective places to look for employment. Known as the

> *Over 80 percent of all jobs are found on the "hidden job market." Only 15 percent of jobs are found on the "advertised job market."*

"advertised job market," because employers pay to have their job vacancies listed in these media, only about 15 percent of individuals find jobs through these channels. Research continues to confirm that most jobs – over 80 percent – are found on the "hidden job market." These jobs are uncovered through word-of-mouth, networking, cold calls, knocking on doors, and direct application. Jobs found on the hidden job market also tend to be better paying, more secure, less competitive, higher quality, and more satisfying than those found on the advertised job market. Advertised jobs are disproportionately highly competitive, difficult-to-fill, and low-paying positions. After all, employers often have to advertise a job because they find it is difficult to fill through other less public means.

TIP #11
Understand the structure of today's
job market.

There are many more or less useful ways to find a job. Some are more effective than others. Will you, for example, primarily respond to job postings in newspapers and on the Internet with a resume, letter, or phone call? What about blasting your resume to thousands of employers and waiting for your phone to ring or your e-mail box to fill up with invitations to numerous job interviews? Ever considered contacting a headhunter, registering with an employment firm, or paying someone to find you a job? What about putting an ad in the newspaper announcing your availability for employment? Perhaps you will network for information, advice, and job leads through friends and referrals. Maybe you'll do some cold calling by telephone or knock on doors. Or perhaps you'll use a very passive approach by posting your resume online and waiting for employers to discover your availability. Day laborers even stand on corners to be picked up by employers for hourly or daily work.

Whichever job finding method you choose will most likely reflect your understanding of the job market and how the employment game is best played. Where do you think most job vacancies can be found? How do employers recruit candidates? What are the best methods for finding a job? Which methods may be a waste of time? If you believe the old work adage that 80 percent of one's time is wasted on nonproductive pursuits and 20 percent tends to be most productive, you'll see similar work patterns when it comes to job hunting. Indeed, since many job seekers don't understand the structure of the job market, they spend an inordinate amount of time looking for jobs in newspapers and on the Internet. While these sources do yield jobs for a few job seekers, they are not the most productive places to look for a job. Smart job seekers devote about 20 percent of the job search time on this advertised job market and 80 percent of their time pursuing more productive channels – informal word-of-mouth channels related to an ongoing prospecting and networking campaign. They understand that the job market remains highly decentralized, fragmented, and unpredictable despite efforts to increasingly centralize it through online job banks and government one-stop career centers. To be most effective they must use a proactive strategy that opens employers' back doors where they learn about job openings before they are announced through the front door. Their strategy helps employers quickly locate qualified candidates before they are forced to go out into the open recruitment market where they will most likely be inundated with resumes, letters, and phone calls from candidates, recruiters, and employment firms. Indeed, the jobs advertised in newspapers and on the Internet may only represent about 20 percent of vacancies available at any given time. Accordingly, to spend 80 percent of your time pursuing 20 percent of the vacancies is not a smart use of your job search time!

Individuals who primarily look to the newspapers and the Internet for jobs assume that these mediums represent a large portion of the job market or they equate these mediums with the job market. Nothing could be further from the truth. These are advertising mediums that make a great deal of money selling classified ads, job postings, and resume database searches to employers. The real job market is anything but centralized around these advertising mediums. Individuals who are good at dealing with uncertainty and managing chaos will be able to navigate the real job market, which is something they must organize around their particular interests, skills, and goals and which has little to do with advertising mediums.

So, where will you look for your next job? How will you best spend 80 percent of your job search time?

TIP #12
Respond to the advertised job market with realistic expectations.

Since we know the advertised job market does not represent a true picture of jobs available at any particular time, it's best to have relatively low expectations of finding a job on this market – maybe a 15 percent chance that you will actually get a job by responding to newspaper and Internet

Your next job will probably come via word-of-mouth through your networking activities.

postings. If you are like many other job seekers, your next job will probably come via word-of-mouth though your networking activities centered on relatives, friends, colleagues, and acquaintances. Do survey and respond to advertised job postings, but don't spend a great deal of time nor develop high hopes of landing a job through these channels.

TIP #13
Incorporate the hidden job market in
your job search.

As we noted in Tip #10, you should spend most of your job search time focused on the hidden job market. If you are devoting more than 30 percent of your time looking for jobs through classified ads and on the Internet, you are most likely wasting a great deal of job search time that could be put to more productive use by engaging in the most effective job search activities, especially networking and informational interviews. Periodically check what percent of your time is spent on the advertised job market. If you discover you are spending more than 30 percent of your time engaged in this market, reorganize your job search so that it is focused on more effective activities. Your goal should be to get as many job interviews as possible – not to send out lots of resumes and letters in the hope of connecting to a few employers. The fastest way to get job interviews is through networking for information, advice, and referrals – proven techniques we outline in *The Savvy Networker, Interview for Success, Haldane's Best Answers to Tough Interview Questions*, and *Change Your Job, Change Your Life* (Impact Publications).

Individuals with not-so-hot backgrounds should spend most of their job search time focused on the hidden job market. Networking and cold-calling activities enable them to be pre-screened by many individuals who will refer them to employers interested in their abilities and skills. Employers found on the hidden job market are less likely to rely on paper qualifications, which often accentuate red flags of applicants with difficult backgrounds. Through networking, you are screened more on the basis of face-to-face meetings and conversations, where what you say and do during the encounters are more important than what you have written in your resume, letters, and applications.

TIP #14
Use the Internet in your job search but
don't become obsessed with it.

When it comes time to find a job, don't fall in love with the Internet. If not used properly, it has the potential to suck up lots of precious job search time as you engage in many nonproductive online activities.

In fact, few job seekers know how to use the Internet properly in their job search. A very seductive medium, the Internet holds more promise than performance when it comes to finding a job. Unfortunately, a disproportionate number of job seekers use the Internet to find employment, believing that employers actually hire over the Internet! Such job seekers spend an inordinate amount of time posting their resume to popular job sites, such as Monster.com, HotJobs.Yahoo.com, and Career Builder.com, and responding to job listings in the hopes of being struck by lightning! Research continues to show that only about 15 percent of all job seekers found their last job by engaging in such online activities that eventually led to job interviews and an offer. The Internet is a wonderful information and communication tool that is best used, in a job search, for (1) conducting research on jobs, employers, companies, and communities; (2) acquiring useful advice

> *Your most productive online activities will relate to research and communication.*

and referrals; and (3) communicating with individuals via e-mail. Indeed, your most productive online activities will relate to research and communication.

While you should post your resume on various employment websites and periodically review online job listings, just don't spend a great deal of time doing so and then waiting to hear from employers based on such activities. Move on to other more productive activities, especially visiting employer websites, which are more likely to yield useful information, job listings, and applications than the more general and popular employment websites.

In fact, since more and more employers recruit directly from their own websites rather than use general employment websites, you are well advised to explore employer websites for job vacancy information. For example, companies such as Microsoft (www.microsoft.com/careers) and Boston Consulting Group (www.bcg.com) provide a wealth of information for job seekers interested in their companies. You can learn a great deal about job hunting by visiting those two websites alone.

But your most useful online job search activity relates to **research**. Thousands of websites can yield useful information for enhancing your job search. For example, use the Internet to explore different occupations (www.bls.gov/oco) and employers (www.hoovers.com), community-based employment assistance (www.careeronestop.org), career counselors (www.nbcc.org), networking groups (www.linkedin.com), salary ranges (www.salary.com), best communities (www.findyourspot.com), relocation (www.moving.com), job search tips (www.winningthejob.com), and career advice (www.wetfeet.com). You can even use the Internet to conduct an online assessment (www.careerlab.com), blast your resume to thousands of employers (www.resumeblaster.com), contact recruiters (www.recruitersonline.com), and explore hundreds of professional associations (www.ipl.org/div/aon) and nonprofit organizations (www.guidestar.org) that are linked to thousands of employers.

For more information on how to wisely use the Internet in your job search, see Ron and Caryl Krannich's *America's Top Internet Job Sites* (Impact Publications), Margaret Dikel's *Job Searching on the Internet* (McGraw-Hill), and Richard Nelson Bolles, *Job Hunting on the Internet* (Ten Speed Press), which are available through Impact Publications (www.impactpublications.com or see the order form at the end of this book).

TIP #15
Approach your job search as a combination paper, electronic, and people process.

Make sure your paper and e-mail products are perfect – error-free and well targeted – since they represent your best efforts to strangers.

In the end, people hire people. Resumes, letters, and applications are screening devices. Employers hire individuals based upon the outcome of face-to-face interviews rather than on the content of their written communications. Therefore, the purpose of your paper, pencil, and typing activities is to make **connections** with the right people who, in turn, will invite you to a job interview based upon the quality of your written communication and possibly a telephone screening interview. Whatever you do, make sure your paper and e-mail products are **perfect** – error-free and well targeted – since they represent your best efforts to strangers whom you need to persuade to invite you to a job interview. The whole networking process, which is the basis for finding the best quality jobs, is primarily a people process – you connect to other individuals by way of telephone calls and face-to-face meetings. How you communicate both verbally and nonverbally will largely determine the outcome of your job search. Be especially attentive to what you say and do when networking and interviewing for a job.

TIP #16
Focus on jobs appropriate for your qualifications.

Many job seekers engage in a great deal of random and wishful thinking activities, such as applying for jobs that have little relationship to their qualifications. When employers look for employees, they try to solve specific problems relating to skills and experience they need. They usually know exactly what they want in terms of qualifications and spell their needs out accordingly. Don't waste your time applying for jobs for which you are not qualified or ones for which you're greatly over-qualified. Try to match your qualifications as closely as

Create a "T" letter that clearly states how your qualifica-tions match the spe-cific requirements for the job.

possible with the requirements of the job. One of the most effective ways to do this to create a "T" letter that clearly states how your qualifications match the specific requirements for the job. Take, for example, the "T" letter on page 36, which can be used in lieu of a resume when applying for a position. This letter emphasizes a one-to-one match between the employer's job requirements and the candidate's qualifications. Employers who receive such letters have little difficulty screening a candidate's qualifications since they are spelled out in the clearest terms possible. Employers usually respond well to such letters since they do not need to spend a great deal of time interpreting a general resume, letter, or application that may be written for many types of employers. Be specific, be targeted, and be responsive whenever you respond to job vacancy announcements.

"T" Letter

July 21, 20 ___

Darlene Compton
Timberlake-Thompson Company
892 Champion Drive
Austin, TX 77889

Dear Ms. Compton:

I'm responding to your job posting that appears on the CampusCareerCenter website for a Public Relations Specialist. My profile is available online (#1234321) with CCC and I e-mailed a copy of my resume to you today as you requested.

I believe I am an excellent candidate for this position given my interests, educational background, and recent internship experience in Public Relations:

Your Requirements	My Qualifications
1+ years of experience in PR	Served as a PR intern during the past three summers with special focus on sales and marketing strategies.
Strong interpersonal skills	Praised by professors and supervisors for working well in teams and with both co-workers and clients. Received the "Intern of the Year" Award in 2001.
Ability to develop compelling ad copy	Developed copy for three ad campaigns which were used in major television and radio spots. Client realized a 30% increase in sales due to these efforts.
Energetic and willing to travel	Work well with deadlines and stressful situations. "Energy and enthusiasm" cited as major characteristics in receiving the internship award. Love to travel.

In addition, I know the importance of building strong customer relations and developing innovative approaches to today's new PR mediums. I love taking on new challenges, working in multiple team and project settings, and seeing clients achieve results from my company's efforts.

I believe there is a strong match between your needs and my professional interests and qualifications. Could we meet soon to discuss how we might best work together? I'll call your office Tuesday at 11am to see if your schedule might permit such a meeting.

I appreciate your consideration and looking forward to speaking with you on Tuesday.

Sincerely,

Sterling Richards

Sterling Richards

TIP #17
Always communicate with a language that is positive, energetic, and enthusiastic.

Employers want to hire energetic and enthusiastic people they like. Such people have a positive attitude (see Tip #5) about their job, work, and future. They tend to be productive people who work well with others. Despite occasional ups and downs, make sure you maintain a positive attitude throughout your job search as well as on the job. Accept rejections as part of the job search. Be persistent and continue to move on expecting you will encounter acceptances.

While your resume and applications generally follow a standard format for presenting qualifications, your job search letters and e-mail provide opportunities for you to express your personality. Choose language that expresses a positive attitude, energy, and enthusiasm. You can energize your resume and job search letters by using action verbs and the active voice. Avoid the passive voice, which tends to remove you from action and make you sound less than enthusiastic. If your grammar rules are a bit rusty, here are some examples of action verbs:

administered	investigated
analyzed	managed
assisted	negotiated
communicated	organized
conducted	planned
coordinated	proposed
created	recommended
designed	recruited
developed	reduced
directed	reorganized
established	revised
evaluated	selected
expanded	streamlined
generated	supervised
implemented	trained
increased	trimmed
initiated	wrote

When applied to the active voice, action or transitive verbs follow a particular grammatical pattern:

Subject	Action Verb	Direct Object
I	increased	profits
I	initiated	studies
I	expanded	production

However, omit the subject (I) if listing your accomplishments. If written in the passive voice versus the active voice, these examples would appear in the "Experience" section of a resume in the following form:

Passive Voice (Don't)	Active Voice (Do)
Profits were increased by 32 percent.	Increased profits by 32 percent.
The studies resulted in new legislation.	Initiated studies that resulted in new legislation.
Production was expanded by 24 percent.	Expanded production by 24 percent.

Avoid using the passive voice since it diminishes your value. With the passive voice, readers aren't sure what you did versus what others in your company or organization did. If you use action verbs and the active voice, you can clearly write about **your** accomplishments and inject energy into your writing. Action verbs imply that you, the subject, performed the action. The reader will know **you** were in charge and got things done.

When you inject energy, enthusiasm, and personality into your writing, you inform the reader that you are not the typical job seeker who is going through the mechanics of applying for a job. Contrast, for example, these two job search letters which are important in a networking campaign for generating informational interviews:

Letter #1

Janice Walker recommended that I write to you concerning my interest in landscape architecture. I would appreciate an opportunity to discuss possible job opportunities for someone with my background. I'm enclosing my resume for your reference. I look forward to hearing from you.

Letter #2

Janice Walker was right. Your work at Meadows Fields was brilliant. I know because I closely watched the landscape changes that took place there when I was working for R.C. Associates. In fact, borrowing from your innovative retainer wall design that incorporated the use of both stone and timber materials, we were able to develop an award-winning design for the new Jenkins Park on Olivia Reservoir. I also was able to develop a series of attractive ponds and fountains that quickly became models for several commercial projects.

I'm excited about the possibility of doing similar work with a company that would be interested in my unique approach to several architectural elements which I've developed over the past six months. Could we meet? I will call you Tuesday morning.

Which letter appeals to you more? While both of these approach letters begin with a personal connection to Janice Walker, the remainder of the letters are quite different. The first letter is the typical formal letter of introduction most job seekers write. It tells you nothing about the writer other than his asking for the recipient's help in his job search – perhaps obligatory (because of a personal connection) but time-consuming encounter that most people would like to avoid. The second letter is different and stands out as special. It speaks directly to the interests of the recipient. Best of all, it expresses a genuine sense of energy and enthusiasm. Chances are the reader will be impressed with the second letter, which appears to be written by a very interesting and talented individual, and may actually want to meet with the writer.

Words such as "delighted," "excited," "happy," "enjoy," and "look forward" tend to communicate a positive attitude. Talking about skills, accomplishments, and performance emphasizes action and outcomes. Whether you are writing, talking over the telephone, or in a face-to-face interview, choose words and phrases that emphasize your energy and enthusiasm. For excellent compendiums of positive keywords and phrases to use in your job search, see Wendy S. Enelow's *Best KeyWords for*

Resumes, Cover Letters, and Interviews and *KeyWords to Nail Your Job Interview* (Impact Publications), which are available through the order form at the end of this book.

TIP #18
Despite periodic rejections, keep enthusiastic and motivated throughout your job search.

Let's face it. Few people can maintain the same level of energy, enthusiasm, and motivation throughout a three- to six-month job search. It's especially difficult when they encounter numerous rejections along the way. Indeed, the number one problem most job seekers encounter and have difficulty dealing with is rejections. Accustomed to being successful in other aspects of their lives, they find a job search can be very ego deflating and depressing. In fact, most people

> *The number one problem most job seekers encounter and have difficulty dealing with is rejections.*

can handle three rejections in a row, but four, five, six, or seven rejections are difficult to deal with. Faced with a string of rejections, many job seekers become demoralized, cut back on their job search activities, or just go through the motions of looking for a job by sending out more resumes and letters in response to classified ads and online job postings.

But there are certain things you can do to keep yourself focused and motivated. First, treat rejections as part of the game. You can't get acceptances before acquiring numerous rejections. Consider the typical job search which goes something like this:

No, No, No, No, No, No, Maybe, No, No, No, Yes, No, No, No
No, No, No, Maybe, No, Maybe, Yes, No, No, No, No, Yes, Yes

If you get disillusioned and quit after receiving four rejections, you will prematurely fail. You need to continue "collecting" more rejections in order to get an acceptance. In fact, we often recommend that individuals get up in the morning with the idea of collecting at least 20 rejections! You will eventually get acceptances, but you must first deal with many rejections on the road to success. How you handle rejections may largely determine how successful you will be in your job search, career, and life.

If you identify what it is you want to do but cannot implement the necessary changes because you fear rejection, you will be going nowhere with your future.

Second, reward yourself after achieving certain goals. For example, let's say your goal this week is to send out 20 resumes, make 35 networking calls, and arrange four informational interviews. If you start on Monday and achieve these goals by Thursday, reward yourself by taking Friday off or go out for dinner at your favorite restaurant. Try to build a system of rewards related to specific goals so that you can occasionally celebrate successes. These little rewards will help keep you focused and motivated throughout your job search. Remember, this is a process that takes time and requires a positive approach to rejections.

Third, if you become depressed and find it difficult to get motivated and active in your job search, take a few days off and engage in some useful volunteer work to recharge your batteries. Helping other people deal with their problems – be it housing, hunger, employment, or illness – will give you a different perspective on life. Chances are it will provide a fresh perspective on your situation and help motivate you to get back on track with your job search. Indeed, changing your environment by associating with different people and situations can be refreshing.

TIP #19
Don't make unnecessary assumptions
about the job market and employers.

Many job seekers believe in numerous myths about the job market and employers that prevent them from becoming successful. Some of the most common myths include:

- Finding a job won't take long since I have a great deal of experience.

- I should be able to significantly increase my income in my next job.

- The best way to find a job is to respond to classified ads, use employment agencies, and submit applications to personnel offices.

- Few jobs are available for me in today's job market.

- Employers are in the driver's seat; they have the upper hand with applicants.

- Employers hire the best qualified candidates.

- It's best to go into a growing field where jobs are plentiful.

- People over 40 have difficulty finding a good job.

- It's best to use an employment firm to find a job.

- I must be aggressive in order to find a job.

- I should not use "connections" to get a job.

- Once I apply for a job, it's best to wait to hear from an employer.

- A good resume is the key to getting a job.

- Salaries are pre-determined by employers.

- It's best to broadcast or "shotgun" my resume to as many employers and recruiters as possible.

Believing in any of these myths will most likely slow down your job search. These and many other myths are outlined in our *High Impact Resumes and Letters* and *Change Your Job, Change Your Life* (Impact Publications).

TIP #20
Check the quality of your writing, interpersonal communication, and public speaking skills.

Employers look for reasons to both reject and accept you. They want to know why they should or should not hire you. They look for any suspicious red flags that may indicate you are the wrong fit for the job and their organization. They do this by carefully looking at how you communicate and interact with them, whether it be on paper, over the Internet, on the telephone, or in a face-to-face interview setting.

Finding a job is all about communicating your qualifications to employers, who, for the most part, are strangers. Communication comes in many forms and through several mediums. In the job search, the most critical communications are written, telephone, and face-to-face conversations which have both verbal and nonverbal elements. What you say and how you say it are equally important. In fact, over 80 percent of communication in a job search will be nonverbal. Employers examine resumes, letters, and applications for behavioral clues. Regardless of the actual content of your resume or letter, if you misspell words, make punctuation and grammatical errors, use an unattractive format, or address the recipient incorrectly, such mistakes say something about your qualifications or lack thereof. Indeed, you may be perceived as more trouble than you are worth and thus not worthy of being invited to a job interview. If you use poor grammar and are evasive and negative over the telephone, you will probably be screened out for a face-to-face interview. If you arrive at your job interview late, wear excessive jewelry, lack good eye contact, give incomplete answers, bad-mouth previous employers, stumble over behavioral and situational questions, and fail to raise thoughtful questions and close the interview properly, you will probably be eliminated from further consideration.

Employers want to work with individuals who are good and effective communicators. Indeed, communication skills – writing, interpersonal, and public speaking – rank very high on employers' lists of most desirable skills in employees, often ahead of specific technical skills. If your communication skills need improvement, by all means seek help. Contact an adult education program through your local school district or a community or junior college for assistance. You'll find various courses, from basic reading, spelling, vocabulary, grammar, and listening, to computer, business writing, and public speaking, available through such programs and colleges. These skills are key to finding good jobs, getting ahead on the job, and advancing careers. They will follow you throughout your worklife. In fact, giving a speech is ranked as the number one fear – outranking death, which is number six! Most important of all, each year thousands of individuals pass up promotions because of the fear of giving briefings, presentations, and speeches that normally go with many promotions. If you are a reluctant communicator, consider joining one of the many Toastmasters groups for developing presentation skills in a non-threatening, supportive environment (www.toastmasters.org or 1-800-993-7732) as well as acquire a copy of Caryl Krannich's *101 Secrets of Highly Effective Speakers* (Impact Publications).

It's imperative that you carefully check the quality of your communication at every stage of your job search. Be very careful what you say and how you say it since employers are looking for cues to eliminate you from consideration.

TIP #21
Seek professional help if necessary –
don't play Lone Ranger all the time.

Many job seekers believe they can conduct a job search on their own. Just write a resume and send it to several employers; within a few days their phone should start ringing and they will be interviewed and offered a job. In reality, the job search is more complicated and unpredictable. While a resume is important for presenting qualifications to employers, the job interview is by far the most important element to landing a job. No resume, no interview; no interview, no job offer. At the same time, it may take three to six months to find the right job. During that time, most job seekers encounter numerous disheartening rejections that often diminish their energy and enthusiasm. Our experience is that fewer than 20 percent of all job seekers can effectively conduct a job search on their own just by following the advice of career experts. The successful individuals tend to be self-starters who are very focused and motivated. The remaining 80 percent of job seekers can benefit from some form of assistance from career counselors, coaches, or a support group. Having someone to work with and share your experience with, including the inevitable ups and downs, can help immensely in moving your job search ahead. In fact, many job seekers can cut their job search time in half by working with a professional or support group. A career professional can be especially helpful at certain critical stages of

> *When shopping for a career professional, never sign a contract before you read the fine print, get a second opinion, and talk to former clients about **results**.*

your job search, especially in conducting a self-assessment, writing resumes, and preparing for interviews. Starting on the next page are some of the most important sources and services for acquiring professional assistance. Each of these services has certain advantages and disadvantages. Approach them with caution. Since career planning is a big and largely unregulated business, you will occasionally encounter hucksters and fraudulent services aimed at taking advantage of individuals who are psychologically vulnerable, anxious, and naive. Many of these hucksters self-certify themselves, promise to locate jobs that pay more than your last one, and seal the deal by asking for up-front money – $500 to $15,000 – to find you a job. Lacking good shopping sense, engaging in wishful thinking, and vulnerable in this rather confusing and often depressing process, many job seekers fall for the false promises of these so-called employment experts.

Our advice is very simple: **Never** sign a contract before you read the fine print, get a second opinion, and talk to former clients about the **results** they achieved through the service. While most of these services are not free, there is no reason to believe that the most expensive services are the best services. In fact, you may get the same quality of services from a group that charges $300 versus one that costs much more. At the same time, free or cheap services are not necessarily as good as the more expensive services. While you often get what you pay for in this industry, you also may get much less than what you pay for! Again, before using any employment services or hiring an expert, do your research by asking for references and contacting individuals who have used the services.

With these words of caution in mind, let's examine a variety of services available, some of which you may want to incorporate in your career planning and job search efforts.

1. Public employment services

Public employment services usually consist of a state agency which provides employment assistance as well as pays unemployment compensation benefits. Employment assistance largely consists of job listings and counseling services. However, counseling services often screen individuals for employers who list with the public employment agency. If you are looking for an entry-level job or a job paying $18,000 to $40,000, contact these services. However, most employers still do not list with them, especially for positions paying more than $40,000 a year. Although the main purpose of these offices has been to dispense unemployment benefits, don't overlook them because of past stereotypes. The Workforce Development Act has re-energized such services. Within the past five years, many of these offices have literally "reinvented" themselves for today's job market as One-Stop Career Centers, offering computerized job banks, counseling services, training programs, and other innovative organizational and technical approaches. Many of them offer useful employment services, including self-assessment and job search workshops as well as access to job listings on the Internet. Most of these offices are linked to America's Job Bank (www.ajb.dni.us), a huge electronic job bank which includes over 1 million job listings throughout the U.S. and abroad. This is one of the premier employment websites with a wealth of information and resources. America's Job Bank, in turn, is linked to the U.S. Department of Labor's three other useful websites – America's CareerInfoNet (www.acinet.org), America's Service Locator (www. servicelocator.org), Career OneStop (www.careeronestop.org), and Career Voyages (www.careervoyages. org). If you are a veteran, you will find many of the jobs listed with state employment offices give veterans preference in hiring. Go see for yourself if your state employment office offers useful services for you.

2. Private employment agencies

Private employment agencies work for money, either from applicants or employers. Approximately 8,000 such agencies operate nation-wide. Many are highly specialized in technical, scientific, and financial fields. The majority of these firms serve the interests of employers, since employers – not applicants – represent repeat business. While employers normally pay the placement fee, many agencies charge applicants 10 to 15 percent of their first year salary. These firms have one major advantage: job leads which you may have difficulty uncovering elsewhere. Especially for highly specialized fields, a good firm can be extremely helpful. The major disadvantages are that they can be costly and the quality of the firms varies. Be careful in how you deal with them. Make sure you understand the fee structure and what they will do for you before you sign anything.

3. Temporary staffing firms

During the past decade temporary staffing firms have come of age as more and more employers turn to them for recruitment assistance. They offer a variety of employment services to both applicants and employers who are either looking for temporary work and workers or who want to better screen applicants and employers. Many of these firms, such as Manpower (www.manpower.com), Olsten (www. olsten.com), and Kelly Services (www.kellyservices.com), recruit individuals for a wide range of positions and skill levels as well as full-time employment. Some firms, such as Robert Half International (www.rhii.com), specialize in certain types of workers, such as accounting, law, information technology, and computer personnel. If you are interested in "testing the job waters," you may want to contact these firms for information on their services. Employers – not job seekers – pay for these services. While many of these firms are listed in your community Yellow Pages, most have websites. The following websites are especially popular with individuals interested in part-time, temporary, or contract work: www.net-temps.com, www.elance.com, www.ework.com, www.guru.com, and www.talent market.monster.com.

4. College/university placement offices

College and university placement offices provide in-house career planning services for graduating students. While some give assistance to alumni, don't expect too much help if you have already graduated; you may, instead, need to contact the alumni office which may offer employment services. Many college placement offices are understaffed or provide only rudimentary services, such as maintaining a career planning library, coordinating on-campus interviews for graduating seniors, and conducting workshops on how to write resumes and interview. Others provide a full range of well supported services including testing and one-on-one counseling. Indeed, many community colleges offer such services to members of the community on a walk-in basis. You can use their libraries and computerized career assessment programs, take personality and interest inventories, or attend special workshops or full-semester career planning courses which will take you through each step of the career planning and job search processes. You may want to enroll in such a course since it is likely to provide just enough structure and content to assess your motivated abilities and skills and to assist you in implementing a successful job search plan. Check with your local campus to see what services you might use.

Many of the college and university placement offices belong to the National Association of Colleges and Employers, which operates its own employment website: www.jobweb.com. This site includes a wealth of information on employment for college graduates (see the "Site Map" section: www.jobweb.com/search/sitemap.htm). Its "Career Library" section includes direct links to hundreds of college and university placement offices: www.jobweb.com/Career_Develop ment/collegeres.htm. To find college alumni offices, visit the following websites: www.alumni.net, www.bcharrispub.com, and www.jobweb.com/After_College. Since colleges and universities tend to be very web-savvy, you can visit hundreds of their career websites to acquire all types of useful free information on conducting an effective job search. One of our favorites is the website operated by the Career Center at the College of William and Mary (www.wm. edu/career). Indeed, searching many of these college and university websites is comparable to having your own personal career counselor – without having to go to college!

5. Private career and job search firms

Private career and job search firms help individuals acquire job search skills and coach them through the process of finding a job. They do not find you a job. In other words, they teach you much of what is outlined in this book. Expect to pay anywhere from $1,500 to $10,000 for this service. If you need a structured environment for conducting your job search, contract with one of these firms for professional assistance. One of the major such firms used to be Bernard Haldane Associates (they ceased operating under that name and became BH Careers International, www.bhcareers.com, in 2004). Many of their pioneering career planning and job search methods are incorporated in this book as well as can be found in five other key job search books: *Haldane's Best Resumes for Professionals, Haldane's Best Cover Letters for Professionals, Haldane's Best Answers to Tough Interview Questions, Haldane's*

Best Salary Tips for Professionals, and *Haldane's Best Employ-ment Websites for Professionals* (Impact Publications – see the order form at the end of this book or www.impactpublications.com). Other firms offering similar services include Right Management Associates (www.right.com), R. L. Stevens & Associates (www.inter viewing.com), and Lee Hecht Harrison (www.lhh.com/us).

6. Executive search firms and headhunters

Executive search firms work for employers seeking candidates to fill critical positions in the $50,000 plus salary range. They also are called "headhunters," "management consultants," and "executive recruiters." These firms play an important role in linking high level technical and managerial talent to organizations. Don't expect to contract for these services. Executive recruiters work for employers, not applicants. If a friend or relative is in this business or you have relevant skills of interest to these firms, let them know you are avail-able – and ask for their advice. On the other hand, you may want to contact firms that specialize in recruiting individuals with your skill specialty. For a comprehensive listing of these firms, see the latest annual edition of *The Directory of Executive Recruiters* (Kennedy Information, www.kennedyinfo.com; also see the order form at the end of this book or www.impactpublications.com). Several com-panies, such as www.resumezapper.com, www.blastmyresume.com, and www.resumeblaster.com, offer e-mail resume blasting services that primarily target headhunters. For a fee, which usually ranges from $50 to $200, these firms will blast your resume to 5,000 to 10,000 headhunters. This is a quick, easy, and inexpensive way to reach thousands of headhunters and executive search firms. This resume distribution method also may be a waste of time and money. Approach it with a sense of healthy skepticism.

7. Marketing services

Marketing services represent an interesting combination of job search and executive search activities. They can cost $2,500 or more, and they work with individuals anticipating a starting salary of at least $75,000 but preferably over $100,000. These firms try to minimize the time and risk of applying for jobs. A typical operation begins with a client paying a $150 fee for developing psychological, skills, and interests profiles. If you pass this stage – most anyone with money does – you go on to the next one-on-one stage. At this point, a marketing plan is outlined and a contract signed for specific services. Work for the client usually involves activities centered on the resume and interviewing. Using word processing software, the firm normally develops a slick "professional" resume and sends it by mail or e-mail, along with a cover letter, to hundreds – maybe thousands – of firms. Clients are then briefed and sent to interview with interested employers. While you can save money and achieve the same results on your own, these firms do have one major advantage: They save you **time** by doing most of the work for you. Again, approach these services with caution and with the knowledge that you can probably do just as well – if not better – on your own by following the step-by-step advice of this and other job search books.

8. Women's centers and special career services

Women's centers and special career services for displaced workers, such as 40-Plus Clubs (www.40plus.org/links) and Five O'Clock Clubs (www.fiveoclockclub.com), have been established to respond to the employment needs of special groups. Women's centers are particularly active in sponsoring career planning workshops and job information networks. These centers tend to be geared toward elementary job search activities, because many of their clientele consist of homemakers who are entering or re-entering the workforce with little knowledge of the job market. Special career services arise at times for different categories of employees. For example, unemployed aerospace engineers, teachers, veterans, air traffic controllers, and government employees have formed special groups for developing job search skills and sharing job leads.

9. Testing and assessment centers

Testing and assessment centers provide assistance for identifying vocational skills, interests, and objectives. Usually staffed by trained professionals, these centers administer several types of tests and charge from $200 to $900 per person. If you use such services, make sure you are given one or both of the two most popular and reliable tests: *Myers-Briggs Type Indicator®* and the *Strong Interest Inventory®*. You should find both tests helpful in better understanding your interests and decision-making styles. In many cases, the career office at your local community college or women's center can administer these tests at minimum cost ($20 to $40). At the same time, many of these testing and assessment services are now available online. Check out these popular websites: www.skillsone. com, www.self-directed-search.com, www.careerlab.com, www.person alityonline.com, www.assessment.com, and www.personalitytype. com.

10. Job fairs and career conferences

Job fairs and career conferences are organized by a variety of groups – from schools and government agencies to headhunters, employment agencies, and professional associations – to link applicants to employers. **Job fairs** are often open to the public and involve many employers. **Career conferences** may be closed to the public (invitation only) and involve a single employer. Usually consisting of one- to two-day meetings in a hotel or conference center, employers meet with applicants as a group and on a one-to-one basis. Employers give presentations on their companies, applicants circulate resumes, and employers interview candidates. Many such conferences are organized to attract hard-to-recruit groups, such as engineers, computer programmers, individuals with security clearances, and clerical and service workers, or for special population groups, such as minorities, transitioning military personnel, women, people with disabilities, and even ex-offenders. These are excellent sources for job leads and information on specific employers and jobs – if you are invited to attend or if the meeting is open to the public. Employers pay for this service, although some job fairs and career conferences may charge job seekers a nominal registration fee.

11. Professional associations

Professional associations often provide placement assistance. This usually consists of listing job vacancies in publications, maintaining a resume database, and organizing a job information exchange at annual conferences. Some may even organize job fairs, such as the

Military Officers Association of America (www.moaa.org) and the Non Commissioned Officers Association (www.ncoausa.org). Many large associations operate their own online employment sites; members can include their resume in an electronic database and employers can access the database to search for qualified candidates. Annual conferences are good sources for making job contacts in different geographic locations within a particular professional field. But don't expect too much. Talking to people (networking) at professional conferences may yield better results than reading job listings, placing your resume in a database, or interviewing at conference placement centers. For excellent online directories of professional associations, be sure to visit these two sites: www.ipl.org/ref/aon and www.asaenet.org.

12. Professional resume writers

Professional resume writers are increasingly playing an important role in career planning. Each year thousands of job seekers rely on these professionals for assistance in writing their resumes. Many of these professionals also provide useful job search tips on resume distribution, cover letters, and networking as well as include other career planning and job search services, such as assessment, mentoring, coaching, and practice interviewing. Charging from $100 to $600 for writing a resume, they work with the whole spectrum of job seekers – entry-level to senior executives making millions of dollars each year. While some are certified career counselors, many of these professionals have their own associations and certification groups that include a large assortment of often unintelligible initials after their names – CAC, CBC, CCM, CEIP, CHRE, CIPC, CPC, CPRW, JCTC, LPC, NBCC, NCC, NCCC, NCRW, and PCC. If you are interested in working with a professional resume writer, visit the following websites for information on this network of career professionals: www.parw.com, www.prwra.com, www.cminstitute.com, and www.nrwaweb.com. Examples of their high-end work can be found in our *High Impact Resumes and Letters* and *Nail the Resume* as well as in Wendy Enelow's resume books: *Best Resumes for $100,000+ Jobs, Best Cover Letters for $100,000+ Jobs, Best Career Transition Resumes for $100,000+ Jobs,* and *Executive Job Search for $100,000 to $1 Million+ Jobs* (Impact

Publications – see order form at the end of this book or visit the publisher's online bookstore: www.impactpublications.com).

13. Certified Career Professionals

Certified career professionals are experienced in working one-on-one with clients, with special emphasis on career assessment. They have their own professional associations. If you are interested in contacting a certified career professional for assistance, we advise you to first visit these websites for locating a career professional:

- **National Board for Certified Counselors, Inc.**   www.nbcc.org

- **National Career Development Association**   www.ncda.org

- **Certified Career Coaches**   www.certifiedcareercoaches.com

- **Career Planning and Adult Development Network**   www.careernetwork.org

You also can find a great deal of professional career assistance through the U.S. Department of Labor's website, which enables users to locate services within their communities:

- **America's Service Locator**   www.servicelocator.org

Whatever you do, be a smart shopper for career planning and job search services. Proceed with caution, know exactly what you are getting into, and choose the best. Remember, there is no such thing as a free lunch, and you often get less than what you pay for. At the same time, the most expensive services are not necessarily the best. Indeed, the free and inexpensive career planning services offered by many community or junior colleges – libraries, computerized career assessment programs, testing, and workshops – may be all you need. On the other hand, don't be afraid to spend some money on getting the best services for your needs. You may quickly discover that this money was well spent when you land a job that pays 20 to 40 percent more than your previous job! Whatever you do, don't be *"pennywise but pound foolish"* by trying to do your job search on the cheap. If you have difficulty writing a first-class resume, by all means contact a resume-writing pro who can put together a dynamite resume that truly represents what you have done, can do, and will do in the future.

After completing this book, you should be able to make intelligent decisions about what, when, where, and with what results you can use professional assistance. Shop around, compare services and costs, ask questions, talk to former clients, and read the fine print before giving an employment expert a job using your hard-earned money. Don't try to be the Lone Ranger all of the time. If necessary, contact a career professional at different stages of your job search. A career expert could very well become your best friend for deciding exactly what you want to do in the future!

> *The free and inexpensive career planning services offered by many community colleges – libraries, testing, and workshops – may be all you need.*

TIP #22
Select your references very carefully.

Employers are suspicious of strangers, which means most job seekers. Many are rightfully suspicious because they have previously encountered problems with candidates who have misrepresented their qualifications. In fact, research has found that nearly 70 percent of job seekers lie on their resumes. As a result of bad hiring decisions, employers increasingly "google" candidates, conduct background checks, and follow through on references provided by candidates. A thorough background check may uncover everything from your employment history and housing situation to credit history and any criminal activity. If, for example, you have been convicted of a crime, chances are that conviction will be revealed during a routine background check. As many ex-offenders quickly discover, there are few places to hide these days given the use of computerized databases and background checks.

In addition to contacting previous employers, many employers will ask for a list of references and then check them accordingly. While many previous employers will only verify employment and attendance records, many employers and references will respond to this often-asked and revealing question posed by reference checkers:

> *"Knowing what you do about this individual, would you hire him again today?"*

A definite "Yes" is a strong recommendation. A "No," "Maybe," "Not sure," or "I'd rather not answer such questions" could raise red flags in the mind of a prospective employer. Therefore, it's very important that you choose your references wisely and contact them as well as previous employers (those who employed you during the past 10 years only) about your impending job change. Send these individuals a copy of your resume along with an explanation of your current employment situation, interests, and skills. Not only is this a wise thing to do, it's also a very professional and thoughtful action on your part. You don't want a prospective employer contacting a previous employer or reference and receive this response:

> *"Oh, I didn't know he was looking for a job again. What's he up to these days?"*

Instead, you want the individual to speak authoritatively about you, your accomplishments and character, and how you might be perfect for this job:

> *"Yes, I would delighted to tell you about him. This job sounds like a perfect fit for both you and Tom."*

Many individuals you contact as references also may play important roles in your network. Consider this an important networking activity that may result in useful advice and referrals.

TIP #23
Ask good questions.

Conducting an effective job search requires asking lots of questions of many individuals. You need to be curious about jobs, employers, organizations, skills, opportunities, and other important aspects of finding and keeping a job if you are to make intelligent decisions concerning your future. After all, not only do you want to impress upon employers that you are the right person for the job, which you do when you ask questions, you also need information to determine if you want to work for particular employers. Much of your job search should involve **research** – gathering information from others about different jobs, employers, companies, communities, and salaries and benefits. You need to learn who has the power to hire, how you can best approach a company for a job, and what it is like working for particular organizations and individuals. You'll especially want to ask questions during job interviews. Develop a list of questions you should ask of employers. For a good introduction to the type of questions you should ask at a job interview, see Richard Fein's *101 Dynamite Questions to Ask At Your Job Interview* (Impact Publications).

TIP #24
Be a good listener.

Listening is an active skill that can be learned. Being a good listener takes effort. It requires active involvement. One of the major errors job seekers make is talking too much and listening too little. Especially during job interviews, employers are turned off by candidates who constantly talk but seem not to be interested in listening to what the interviewer or others are saying. Since most people interpret no response as a negative response, avoid an expressionless face when listening to others. Try to become a good listener by acquiring several nonverbal behaviors associated with active listening:

- Focus on what is being said rather than thinking about how the other person looks, what you want to say next, or your nervousness or fear of not getting a job offer.

- Listen objectively for content and avoid being distracted by any annoying words, ideas, or mannerisms of others.

- Try to listen for information and withhold evaluation of the message until later.

- Give positive feedback by occasionally nodding in agreement and smiling, which are indications of interest on your part in the speaker and what is being said.

If you try to concentrate on what is being said rather than on how you are doing, you will probably make a good impression on other people. Being other-directed with your nonverbal communication will make you seem more likable and competent than candidates who are noticeably self-concerned and nervous throughout the interview.

TIP #25
Be prepared to handle rejections with a positive attitude and a purposeful plan of action.

As we noted in Tip #18, rejections are a big part of any job search. Everyone encounters them – not just people with red flags in their backgrounds. How you handle rejections may determine how successful you are in finding the right job for you. If you become discouraged because of rejections, you'll have difficulty keeping motivated, maintaining a positive attitude, and taking appropriate actions for advancing your job search. But if you know you need to experience many rejections before encountering a single acceptance, you should be able to develop a plan of action that keeps you focused on achieving your goals. One of the best ways to handle rejections and stay motivated is to join a job search club or form your own support group. Working with others will help you maintain a positive attitude and focus on getting a few important acceptances – invitations to job interviews – as you navigate through a sea of rejections. One of the most important ways to minimize rejections is to develop an active networking campaign involving informational interviews – interviews you conduct to gather information, advice, and referrals. If approached properly, over 50 percent of individuals you ask for an informational interview will agree to speak and/or meet with you. That's a much higher acceptance rate than you will get from sending resumes or completing applications in response to job vacancies. Many informational interviews also lead to actual job interviews and offers. For information on how to minimize rejections through networking and informational interviews, see our *The Savvy Networker* and *Haldane's Best Answers to Tough Interview Questions* (Impact Publications).

TIP #26
Identify any red flags that could be
potential job knockouts.

We all have red flags in our backgrounds. What are yours? Perhaps you dropped out of school, failed an important test, lost a job, experienced financial difficulties, got divorced, became seriously ill, have a physical or mental illness, lack experience and goals, have a criminal record, abused drugs or alcohol, don't relate well to others, appear over-qualified, have work-related problems and poor references, have a learning disorder or physical handicap, or are a job hopper with an unstable work history. Most red flags relate to health, legal, financial, personal, learning, and behavioral problems in your past. For employers, such red flags reveal potential on-the-job problems they would prefer to avoid. If you have any red flags in your background that are likely to become employment issues, you need to deal with these **before** they become potential knock-outs on resumes, in job interviews, or on the job.

If you have ever been fired for the following high-risk behaviors, you have red flags in your background which may eliminate you from consideration for a job should the employer learn about them from your references or a background check:

1. Absent and tardy
2. Broke rules
3. Insubordinate
4. Lying
5. Stealing
6. Uncooperative
7. Drug and alcohol abuse
8. Fighting on the job
9. Bad attitude
10. Dishonest
11. Incompetent
12. Abuse co-workers or clients
13. Unpredictable behavior
14. Lazy and undependable

Respond to the following statements to determine how "not-so-hot" your background may be. Circle the numbers to the right of each statement that best represents your degree of agreement or disagreement:

1 = Strongly agree   4 = Disagree
2 = Agree   5 = Strongly disagree
3 = Uncertain

1. I have little work experience.   1   2   3   4   5

2. I have work experience, but it is very different from what I want to do.   1   2   3   4   5

3. My grades in school were not very good.   1   2   3   4   5

4. I lack a high school diploma or GED.   1   2   3   4   5

5. I did not go to college or I dropped out of college.   1   2   3   4   5

6. I have been fired from one job.   1   2   3   4   5

7. I have been fired from more than one job.   1   2   3   4   5

8. I have held several jobs in the last three years.   1   2   3   4   5

9. The jobs I have held have been very different from each other in terms of the work to be done and skills required.   1   2   3   4   5

10. I don't have a past employer who would give me a good reference.   1   2   3   4   5

11. I have been convicted of a felony.   1   2   3   4   5

12. I have a learning disability.   1   2   3   4   5

13. I have difficulty relating to people.   1   2   3   4   5

14. I've experienced some major medical (physical or mental) problems.   1   2   3   4   5

15. I've experienced marital problems.   1   2   3   4   5

16. My financial situation is difficult.   1   2   3   4   5

17. I've abused drugs and/or alcohol.   1   2   3   4   5

18. I have an arrest record.   1   2   3   4   5

19. If an employer knew much about my employment background, I would probably not be hired.   1   2   3   4   5

20. If an employer knew much about my personal
     background, I would probably not be hired.   1   2   3   4   5

21. I appear over-qualified for the work I want
     to do.   1   2   3   4   5

TOTAL

If you circled a "1" or "2" for any of these statements, you may raise a red flag in the eyes of most employers. If your total score is between 26 and 60, you will most likely appear to have a not-so-hot background in the eyes of most employers. You'll need to develop job search strategies to overcome your job market weaknesses.

The first thing you need to do in dealing with red flags is to identify and acknowledge them as potential job knock-outs. Denying them or making excuses will not help you take corrective actions that can make you more employable. Once you've identified your red flags, the next step is to develop strategies for turning red flags into green flags that tell employers that you will be a good hire. You can start this process by asking yourself the following questions:

1. What questions might an employer ask about my background that could raise red flags about my fitness for the job?

2 What five things about my background could knock me out of consideration for a job?

3. What potential red flag behaviors might I need to re-examine and take greater responsibility for in the future?

4. What positive actions have I taken to change the negative behaviors that raise red flags?

5. Why would someone want to hire me?

6. What are my best work characteristics?

For more information on potential red flags affecting a job search and how to best deal with them, see Caryl and Ron Krannich, *Job Interview Tips for People With Not-So-Hot Backgrounds* (Impact Publications).

TIP #27
Expect the unexpected.

Plan as much as you want but be prepared for the unexpected as well as that wonderful experience called **serendipity**. If your initial plans seem to go awry, don't worry about it since you may be on a more productive yet unpredictable path to job search success. Indeed, if you use a **networking approach** that involves doing research with numerous individuals who are knowledgeable about the job

> *Plan as much as you want but be prepared for serendipity.*

market, and who refer you to other knowledgeable individuals, good things will soon begin to happen as you unexpectedly learn about new employment opportunities. The jobs you eventually interview for will most likely look very different from the ones you initially expected to consider. The job and salary you finally accept may well be beyond your initial expectations. Our point here is that you should and can plan for the unexpected by using an approach that puts you in many different places that will yield positive outcomes for you. Luck will surely come your way if you pursue a very proactive job search centered around building, expanding, and nurturing a powerful network of individuals who have your best employment interests in mind.

TIP #28
Follow 20 key principles to job search success.

Success is determined by more than just a good plan getting implemented. We know success is not determined primarily by intelligence, time management, positive thinking, or luck. Based upon experience, theory, research, common sense, and acceptance of some self-transformation principles, we believe you will achieve job search success by following most of these 20 principles:

1. **You should work hard at finding a job:** Make this a daily endeavor and involve your family. Focus on specifics.

2. **You should not be discouraged by setbacks:** You are playing the odds, so expect disappointments and handle them in stride. You will get many "no's" before finding the one "yes" which is right for you.

3. **You should be patient and persevere:** Expect three to six months of hard work before you connect with the right job.

4. **You should be honest with yourself and others:** Honesty is always the best policy. But don't be naive and stupid by confessing your negatives and shortcomings to others.

5. **You should develop a positive attitude toward yourself:** Nobody wants to employ guilt-ridden people with inferiority complexes. Focus on your positive characteristics.

6. **You should associate with positive and successful people:** Finding a job largely depends on how well you relate to others. Avoid associating with negative and depressing people who complain and have a "you-can't-do-it" attitude. Run with winners who have a positive "can-do" outlook on life.

7. **You should set goals:** You should have a clear idea of what you want and where you are going. Without these, you will present a confusing and indecisive image to others. Clear goals direct your job search into productive channels. Setting high goals will help make you work hard in getting what you want.

8. **You should plan:** Convert your goals into action steps that are organized as short-, intermediate-, and long-range plans.

9. **You should get organized:** Translate your plans into activities, targets, names, addresses, telephone numbers, and materials. Develop an efficient and effective filing system and use a large calendar to set time targets, record appointments, and compile useful information.

10. **You should be a good communicator:** Take stock of your oral, written, and nonverbal communication skills. How well do you communicate? Since most aspects of your job search involve communicating with others, and communication skills are one of the most sought-after skills, always present yourself well both verbally and nonverbally.

11. **You should be energetic and enthusiastic:** Employers are attracted to positive people. They don't like negative and depressing people who toil at their work. Generate enthusiasm both verbally and nonverbally. Check on your telephone voice with a friend or relative – it may be more unenthusiastic than your face-to-face voice.

12. **You should ask questions:** Your best information comes from asking questions. Learn to develop intelligent questions that are non-aggressive, polite, and interesting to others. But don't ask too many questions and thereby become a bore.

13. **You should be a good listener:** Being a good listener is often more important than being a good questioner or talker. Learn to improve your face-to-face listening behavior (nonverbal cues) as well as remember and use information gained from others. Make others feel they enjoyed talking with you, i.e., you are one of the few people who actually **listens** to what they say.

14. **You should be civil, which means being polite, courteous, and thoughtful:** Treat "gatekeepers," especially receptionists, like human beings. Avoid being aggressive. Try to be polite, courteous, and gracious. Your social graces are being observed. Remember to send thank you letters – a very thoughtful thing to do in a job search. Even if rejected, thank employers for the "opportunity." They may later have additional opportunities, and they will remember you.

15. **You should be tactful:** Watch what you say to others about people. Don't be a gossip, back-stabber, or confessor.

16. **You should maintain a professional stance:** Be neat in what you do and wear, and speak with the confidence, authority, and maturity of a professional.

17. **You should demonstrate your intelligence and competence:** Present yourself as someone who gets things done and achieves results – a **producer**. Employers generally seek people who are bright, hard working, responsible, communicate well, have positive personalities, maintain good interpersonal relations, are likable, observe dress and social codes, take initiative, are talented, possess expertise in particular areas, use good judgment, are cooperative, trustworthy, and loyal, generate confidence and credibility, and are conventional. In other words, they like people who score in the "excellent" to "outstanding" categories of a performance evaluation.

18. **You should not overdo your job search:** Don't engage in overkill and bore everyone with your "job search" stories. Achieve balance in everything you do. Occasionally take a few days off to do nothing related to your job search. Develop a system of incentives and rewards – such as two non-job search days a week, if you accomplish targets A, B, C, and D.

19. **You should be open-minded and keep an eye open for "luck":** Too much planning can blind you to unexpected and fruitful opportunities. You should welcome serendipity. Learn to re-evaluate your goals and strategies. Seize new opportunities if appropriate.

20. **You should evaluate your progress and adjust:** Take two hours once every two weeks and evaluate your accomplishments. If necessary, tinker with your plans and reorganize your activities and priorities. Don't become too routinized and thereby kill creativity and innovation.

These principles should provide you with an initial orientation for starting your job search. As you become more experienced, you will develop your own set of operating principles that should work for you.

TIP #29
Focus on your achievements or
accomplishments.

Your greatest assets in the eyes of employers are your achievements or accomplishments – those things you do well and result in important outcomes or benefits for employers and their organizations. Most employers are interested in two types of outcomes – saving money or making money. Whatever you do, avoid what most other job seekers do – primarily focus on their formal duties and responsibilities that normally come with a position. When writing your resume and letters and interview-

> *Employers have two main interests – making money or saving money.*

ing for a job, always stress your major accomplishments. Better still, try to **quantify your accomplishments**. For example, avoid restating your responsibilities in this form:

> I was responsible for maintaining inventory for a 15-employee office supply store.

Instead, state your responsibilities in the form of specific employer-oriented accomplishments:

> Saved XYZ Company $45,000 through improved inventory management over an 18-month period. Installed innovative just-in-time ordering system that reduced returns by 50% and shortened delivery time by 70%.

Statistics that focus on performance send a powerful message to employers about your accomplishments. Whenever possible, communicate your accomplishments in such a form.

TIP #30
Orient yourself to the needs of employers.

Hiring is no fun. After all, employers hire individuals because they need to solve certain problems. If you communicate to employers that you are a problem solver, and you present evidence of related accomplishments, chances are you will be well received and given serious consideration for a job. Whenever possible, try to find out what specific problems an employer is encountering and come up with possible solutions that would benefit the employer. If, for example, you discover an employer's major problem is how to deal with excess ordering, you might propose a computer program you're familiar with that could streamline the ordering process and thus reduce the employer's costs.

The same thing is true when developing your job objective and writing your resume and letters. Make sure they are employer-centered rather than self-centered. While everyone has personal needs and wants to make more money and get ahead, you must not communicate such self-centered needs or greed during your job search. Put yourself in the shoes of the employer: What does he or she most value in a candidate such as you? Once you understand and answer this fundamental question, deciding what to put on your resume and applications as well as on your letters and what to talk about in job interviews becomes relatively self-evident.

TIP #31
Be prepared to be tested by employers.

While you definitely want to assess your interests, skills, and abilities prior to writing your resume, testing and assessment don't end at this initial stage of your job search. More and more employers subject candidates to a variety of tests as part of the screening process. While some may administer tests to learn more about your interests, skills, and abilities, others may also require drug screening and administer psychological tests in order to determine whether or not you fit into their organization or company. Depending on the nature of the job, some candidates may be required to take a

> *More and more employers administer a variety of tests – aptitude, drug, psychological, and even polygraph.*

polygraph examination. Employers also increasingly rely on situational interviews which serve as an additional test – observe how candidates actually perform job-related tasks. If you think you can just write a resume and talk your way to a new job, think again. Employer tests are here to stay and in a very big way. Try to familiarize yourself as much as possible with the types of tests employers are likely to require of you.

While you may not be able to prepare for most such tests, at least be aware that you may have to take tests as a condition of employment. Make sure what you say on your resume and application as, well as in the job interview, is truthful. If not, the tests may indicate otherwise.

TIP #32
Always tell a positive version of the truth.

Honesty is always the best policy when conducting a job search. But honesty does not mean you must confess your weaknesses and talk about your negatives, even though employers would like to know about them. Focus on your strengths and accomplishments but do so truthfully. If you exaggerate your skills and lie about your background, chances are such indiscretions will eventually catch up with you, especially through background checks and testing. Since employers are looking for truthfulness, character, and value in their employees, make sure you communicate such qualities to employers.

TIP #33
Find a job that's fit for you rather than one you think you might fit into.

Most people try to adjust their goals, interests, and skills to fit into the requirements for a particular job. The happiest and most productive workers – those who really love what they do – approach the job market differently. They look for jobs that are a perfect fit for their particular mix of goals, interests, and skills. In so doing, they target their job search on jobs that are right for them.

TIP #34
Always research the job, company, and employer before applying for a position.

Believe it or not, some job seekers go to the job interview and ask the interviewer this killer question: *"What do you do here?"* If you want to make a very bad impression, ask that question. It indicates you didn't do your homework, and you're probably not very interested in the job – just a paycheck. That's inexcusable, especially since information on most employers is readily available on the Internet. Spend a few minutes exploring a company's website and you'll learn a great deal about the company. That information should help you target your resume and cover letter and ask intelligent questions about the company and job during the interview.

Smart job seekers know exactly whom they are dealing with when looking for a job. They research companies and employers **before** sending resumes and letters, completing applications, or going to job interviews. They tailor their resume to respond to the needs of the employer rather than send a generic one-size-fits-all resume. When they go to a job interview, they know a great deal about both the company and employer and have a list of questions prepared to ask the interviewer. These questions indicate they are interested in the job because they are well informed about the company.

TIP #35
Make self-assessment the foundation for
all other job search activities.

As we noted in Tip #2, self-assessment is the foundation step for all other job search activities. Make sure you know what it is you do well and enjoy doing as well as formulate a job objective **before** writing your resume and letters and completing job applications.

Self-assessment information can be invaluable for organizing each phase of your job search. Based on knowledge of your strengths, you should be able to develop a powerful job objective and target your job search on those jobs and employers that best coincide with your interests, skills, and abilities. However, don't become obsessed with or over-rely on such information. Many self-assessment tests and exercises generate very simplistic information that may underwhelm you. If you have a great deal of experience, you may find the *Myers-Briggs Type Indicator®*, *Self-Directed Search®*, *Strong Interest Inventory®*, and *Motivated Skills Exercise* merely confirm what you already know about yourself. In this case, you need to get on with your job search by focusing on communicating your accomplishments to employers. Avoid the temptation of trying to be someone you are not or chasing after glamorous jobs that appeal to you but which do not relate to your foundation interests, skills, and abilities.

TIP #36
Use a variety of approaches to identify your interests, skills, and abilities.

Some job seekers look for a magic bullet – a single test that will reveal all they need to know about themselves, from what career path to choose to the type of job that will make them happy. Indeed, career counselors often encounter such individuals who are frustrated with not knowing what to do with their lives. But there is no such magic bullet when it comes to making career choices. No single test or exercise will reveal enough information to make your job search easy. Each test or exercise looks at one or two major dimensions of human complexity. Some of these devices, for example, only focus on personality and motivation while others examine values, interests, attitudes, skills, behaviors, and aptitudes. The personality approach is by far the most popular and controversial approach.

No one size (test) fits all; you need to try several different testing approaches.

You will find literally hundreds of career tests and exercises designed to help you clarify career choices. For job seekers, this is a bewildering world of testing because of so many alternative choices available. Many job seekers rightfully ask, *"Which test or exercise is best for me?"* Our answer is very simple: No one size fits all; you need to try several different approaches.

We recommend using a variety of approaches that yield different information on yourself, from paper and pencil tests to self-directed exercises. In so doing, you'll gain a great deal of information about yourself, some of which will be confirmed from one test and exercise to another. Here are some of the most popular self-assessment tests, many of which must be administered by certified career counselors and testing experts:

Personality and Motivation Tests

- California Psychological Inventory Form 434 (CPI™ 434)
- Edwards Personal Preference Schedule
- Enneagram
- Keirsey Character Sorter

- Myers-Briggs Type Indicator® (MBTI®)
- 16-Personality Factor Questionnaire (16PF)

Values Tests

- Career Beliefs Inventory (CBI)
- Minnesota Importance Questionnaire (MIQ)
- Survey of Interpersonal Values (SIV)
- Temperament and Values Inventory
- O*NET Career Values Inventory

Interests and Attitudes Tests

- Career Assessment Inventory™ – Enhanced Version (CAI-E)
- Career Exploration Inventory
- Career IQ and Interest Test (CIQIT)
- Guide to Occupational Exploration Interest Inventory
- Harrington-O'Shea Career Decision-Making System
- Jackson Vocational Interest Survey (JVIS)
- Job Search Attitude Inventory (JSAI)
- Kuder Occupational Interest Survey
- Leisure to Occupational Connection Search (LOCS)
- Ohio Vocational Interest Survey
- Self-Directed Search® (SDS)
- Strong Interest Inventory®
- Vocational Interest Inventory

Skills, Behaviors, and Aptitudes Tests

- Barriers to Employment Success Inventory
- BRIGANCE® Diagnostic Employability Skills Inventory
- Career Decision Scale
- FIRO-B®

Multiple Indicators Tests

- APTICOM
- Armed Services Vocational Battery (ASVAB)
- Assessment of Career Decision Making (ACDM)
- The Birkman Method

- CAM Computerized One-Stop
- Campbell™ Interest and Skill Survey (CISS®)
- Career Scope
- Key Educational Vocational Assessment System (KEVAS)
- Vocational Interest, Temperament, and Aptitude System (VITAS)

In addition, you should consider completing several self-directed assessment exercises which can be analyzed on your own rather than with the assistance of a career professional. Some of the most popular such exercises include:

- *The Skills Map* (Richard Nelson Bolles)
- *Autobiography of Accomplishments*
- *Success Factor Analysis* (Bernard Haldane)
- *SIMA* (System for Identifying Motivated Abilities developed by People Management, Inc.)

These and many other tests and exercises are summarized and analyzed in our companion volume, *I Want to Do Something Else, But I'm Not Sure What It Is* (Impact Publications) as well as in several testing directories: *The ETS Test Collection Catalog* (Oryx Press), *Mental Measures Yearbook* (University Nebraska Press), and *Tests* (Pro-Ed).

TIP #37
Understand your motivated abilities
and skills (MAS).

One of the most useful exercises many of our readers use is something we call the "Motivated Skills Exercise." Based on Haldane's "Success Factor Analysis," but sometimes referred to as the "System to Identify Motivated Skills" or "Intensive Skills Exercise," this device focuses on identifying exactly what employers are looking for – your pattern of motivated abilities and skills (MAS). Since employers are looking for **predictable patterns of behavior**, based on the trusted theory that one's future performance is likely to resemble one's past performance, you need to have a clear understanding of your past patterns of behavior. But most important of all, you want to understand what really motivates you to excel – those things you both do well and enjoy doing. The "Motivated

Skills Exercise," which we describe in detail in *I Want to Do Something Else, But I'm Not Sure What It Is,* outlines how to generate such information on yourself within a few hours. It basically involves six steps:

- Identify 15-20 of your major achievements.

- Prioritize your seven most significant achievements.

- Write a full page on each of your prioritized achievements.

- Elaborate on your achievements by having someone interview you by asking "what" and "how" questions.

- Identify patterns by examining the interviewer's notes.

- Synthesize the information by clustering similar skills into categories.

Here's an example of how skills might be grouped into clusters, which identify certain behavioral patterns, or what we call one's motivated abilities and skills (MAS):

Synthesized Skill Clusters

Investigate/Survey/Read Inquire/Probe/Question	Teach/Train/Drill Perform/Show/Demonstrate
Learn/Memorize/Practice Evaluate/Appraise/Assess Compare	Construct/Assemble/Put together
	Organize/Structure/Provide definition/Plan/Chart course
Influence/Involve/Get participation/Publicize Promote	Strategize/Coordinate
	Create/Design/Adapt/Modify

TIP #38
Consider taking the *Myers-Briggs Type Indicator®*, *Self-Directed Search*, and *Strong Interest Inventory®*.

The three most popular assessment devices used in career counseling are the *Myers-Briggs Type Indicator®*, *Self-Directed Search®*, and *Strong Interest Inventory®*. If you decide to take a few counselor-assisted tests, we highly recommend starting with these. Here's what you get:

- **Myers-Briggs Type Indicator® (MBTI):** This is the most popular personality inventory in the world used by psychologists and career counselors. It has multiple applications for everything from marital counseling to executive development programs. Based on Carl Gustav Jung's theory of personality types, this simplified application of his complex theory attempts to measure personality dispositions and interests – the way people absorb information, decide, and communicate. It analyzes preferences to four dichotomies (extroversion/introversion, sensing/intuiting, thinking/feeling, judging/perceiving) which result in 16 personality types. The MBTI comes in a variety of forms. Available through Consulting Psychologists Press (www.cpp.com and www.skillsone.com) and most colleges, universities, and testing centers.

- **Self-Directed Search® (SDS):** One of the most widely used and adapted interest inventories in career counseling. Designed to assist individuals in making career choices based on an analysis of different orientations toward people, data, and things. It matches interests with six types (realistic, investigative, artistic, social, enterprising, and conventional) that are, in turn, related to different occupations that match these types. Used in helping determine how one's interests fit with various occupations. Influential in developing the assessment approach found in Richard Nelson Bolles's *What Color Is Your Parachute?* and *What Color Is Your Parachute Workbook*. Also available in other versions, such as *Self-Directed Search® Career Explorer (SDS CE)* and *Self-Directed Search Form R (SDS Form R)*. Available through Psychological Assessment Resources (www.par inc.com).

■ **Strong Interest Inventory®:** Next to the *Myers-Briggs Type Indicator®* and the *Self-Directed Search®*, this remains one of the most popular assessment devices used by career counselors. Individuals respond to 317 multiple-choice items to determine their occupational interests according to six occupational themes, 25 interest scales, occupational scales, and personal style scales. Used extensively for career guidance, occupational decisions, employment placement, educational choices, and vocational rehabilitation programs. Available through Consulting Psychologists Press (www.cpp.com) and most schools, colleges, universities, and testing centers.

At the same time, you should supplement these paper and pencil tests with some of the self-directed assessment exercises we identified in Tips #35 and #36.

TIP #39
Develop a powerful employer-centered objective.

Many job seekers discover one of the most difficult job search tasks is to develop a job or career objective. This is not something you just create in a few minutes. A basic 25-word objective may take you two or more weeks to develop. You'll draft an initial objective and then further refine it based upon information about your strengths, employers, and jobs. You constantly think about who you are and what you want to really achieve in the future. This process of developing an objective will clear up many fuzzy thoughts as you begin seeing the light at the end of what may initially appear to be a very long tunnel.

> *A basic 25-word objective may take two or more weeks to develop. It will become the most important element in your job search arsenal.*

But once you get your objective right, you'll see how important that objective is to your whole job search as well as your future. As you constantly repeat and refine your objective, you'll discover it's the single most important element in your job search arsenal. Thus, take lots of time to get this initial step right.

TIP #40
Relate your objective to both your interests
and the employer's needs.

Your objective should communicate that you are a **purposeful individual who achieves results**. It can be stated over different time periods as well as at various levels of abstraction and specificity. You can identify short-, intermediate-, and long-range objectives and very general to very specific objectives. Whatever the case, it is best to know your prospective audience before deciding on the type of objective. Your objective should reflect your career interests as well as employers' needs. Examples of different types of objectives at different levels are included in Tip #81.

TIP #41
Make your objective employer-centered rather
than self-centered.

Your objective should be a concise statement of what you want to do and what you have to offer to an employer. The position you seek is "what you want to do"; your qualifications are "what you have to offer." Your objective should state your strongest qualifications for meeting employers' needs. It should communicate what you have to offer an employer without emphasizing what you expect the employer to do for you. In other words, your objective should be **work-centered**, not self-centered; it should not contain trite terms that merely emphasize what you want, such as give me a(n) "opportunity for advancement," "position working with people," "progressive company," or "creative position." Such terms are viewed as "canned" job search language which says little of value about you. Above all, your objective should reflect your honesty and integrity; it should not be "hyped."

TIP #42
Develop a realistic objective.

Objectives should be **realistic**. For example, you may want to become president of the United States or solve all the world's problems. However, these objectives are probably unrealistic. While they may represent your ideals, dreams, and fantasies, you need to be more realistic in terms of what you can personally accomplish in the immediate future given your particular skills, pattern of accomplishments, level of experience, and familiarity with the job market. What, for example, are you prepared to deliver to prospective employers over the next few months? While it is good to set challenging goals, you can overdo it. Refine your objective by thinking about the next major step or two you would like to make in your career advancement. Develop a realistic action plan that focuses on the details of progressing your career one step at a time. Such a plan will allow you to experience success – a key motivator for advancing your career. If you have unrealistic goals, you are likely to experience failure and thus become depressed at being a "loser." By all means avoid making a grandiose leap outside reality!

TIP #43
Make your objective the central organizing principle for implementing your job search.

Your objective should not be limited to just a section on your resume. It should be all encompassing, guiding each phase of your job search. Once you develop a powerful objective, you'll find that all of your other job search activities will fall into place as you focus laser-like on what's most important in your job search in order to achieve your goal. Without such an objective, you may have difficulty deciding what's really important to your job search and thus founder aimlessly in search of jobs that seem interesting to you but which may not relate to your major strengths.

3

Resume Strategies, Issues, and Organization

EVERAL OF OUR TIPS RELATE to key resume strategies or issues surrounding the definition, selection, and organization of various types of resumes. These are **foundation tips** for helping you choose the right type of resume and organize each resume section before actually writing your resume.

TIP #44
Understand the critical role your resume plays in the whole job search process.

The resume plays a **transformational role** in the job search. It moves job seekers from relatively passive and self-centered assessment, research, and writing activities to more interpersonal and face-to-face activities, such as networking and interviewing. As such, the resume should be produced only **after** completing several other job search steps, as indicated in the figure in Tip #2. Unfortunately, many job seekers start their job search by writing their resume prior to conducting a self-assessment and identifying a job objective. The result is often a weak and unfocused resume that quickly turns off prospective employers. Make sure your resume reflects these other job search steps.

TIP #45
Remember the purpose of your resume.

Many job seekers misunderstand the purpose of the resume. Some believe a resume will get them a job, and thus they try to put as much information on their resume as possible. However, the purpose of the resume is to **get invited to a job interview**. Like good advertising copy, it should be designed to persuade the reader to acquire the product, which in this case means inviting a candidate to a job interview. As such, like good advertising copy, the resume needs to be carefully crafted with just enough information to grab the reader's attention and persuade him or her to take action.

TIP #46
Define a resume properly.

What exactly is a resume? It's not a summary of your work history, an autobiography, or an abbreviated version of your biography. It's not something you're writing to your parents or a friend. In its simplest goal-oriented form, a resume is an **advertisement for a job interview**. It's written to persuade prospective employers to invite you to an interview. Once you define a resume in this manner, it's much easier to decide what to include or exclude on your resume. Within the space of one or two pages, you want to include just enough compelling information to grab the attention of the reader, who, in turn, will be sufficiently interested in your qualifications to call you for a job interview. If you define a resume otherwise, chances are you will include lots of extraneous information that will have just the opposite effect – persuade the reader **not** to invite you to an interview!

TIP #47
Make sure you are "resume-ready" before you
start writing your resume.

Just how ready are you to write a resume? Respond to the 12 statements on page 79 to discover your "resume-ready" score:

INSTRUCTIONS: Respond to each statement by circling which number at the right best represents your situation.

SCALE: 1 = Strongly agree   4 = Disagree
                     2 = Agree   5 = Strongly disagree
                     3 = Maybe, not certain

1. I know what I do well and enjoy doing.   1   2   3   4   5

2. I've conducted a self-assessment which identifies my motivated abilities and skills.   1   2   3   4   5

3. I can write a 25-word employer-centered objective.   1   2   3   4   5

4. I can summarize my skills and abilities in less than 25 words.   1   2   3   4   5

5. I can identify three accomplishments for each of my past jobs.   1   2   3   4   5

6. I know what employers are looking for on my resume.   1   2   3   4   5

7. I've taken an inventory of my previous work experience, key skills, and education and training.   1   2   3   4   5

8. I know what keywords to use on my resume.   1   2   3   4   5

9. I know how to customize my resume for different employers.   1   2   3   4   5

10. I know how to evaluate each section of a resume.   1   2   3   4   5

11. I know the best way to distribute my resume.   1   2   3   4   5

12. I know how to best follow up my resume.   1   2   3   4   5

TOTAL   [   ]

If your cumulative score is less than 15 points, you appear well prepared to write and distribute your resume. If you scored higher than 30 points, you have a great deal of resume work ahead of you.

TIP #48
Always write, re-write, and revise your resume
before looking for a job.

"One size fits all" is not a smart way to use your resume. You should try to target your resume for each prospective employer as much as possible. You do this by emphasizing goals and accomplishments that best fit the needs of the employer. If you have a resume that is more than six months old, look it over carefully for ways to strengthen it. Revise and re-write it if necessary. If you are responding to a classified ad or job posting, read it very carefully for clues of what the employer wants. Similar to a "T" Letter (see Tip#16), underline the stated requirements for the job – the keywords, skills, abilities, knowledge, and experience sought. Then examine your resume to make sure it clearly responds to those requirements. In fact, one of the major reasons recruiters reject most resumes is that candidates' paper qualifications do not appear to fit the requirements for the job.

TIP #49
Revise your resume annually, even if you
are not looking for a job.

You should routinely update your resume on an annual basis. In fact, we recommend that everyone do an annual career check-up. Ask yourself if your career goals have changed and what new skills you may have acquired during the past year. Update your accomplishments related to your current job by quantifying what you actually produced for your employer. While you may not be actively looking for a job at present, you need to be job-market prepared should your situation unexpectedly change:

1. Your job changes.
2. Your employer asks you to relocate but you don't want to.
3. Your spouse wants to move and you agree.
4. Your employer falls on hard times as the company declines.

5. You become unhappy with your boss, co-workers, or assignments.
6. You get laid off or fired.
7. You learn about an attractive job opportunity.
8. A friend or recruiter contacts you about an interesting job.

Since jobs and careers are often unpredictable, keep your resume both current and handy. You never know when you might need to use it. If, for example, a recruiter or friend calls you tomorrow about a job they want you to consider, will you have to start writing your resume or do you have one that is already up-to-date and ready to e-mail within minutes?

TIP #50
Strategize how your resume can best relate to a cover letter and job interviews.

Your resume should be viewed as part of other key activities within your larger job search. As such, it needs to be related to cover letters and job interviews. Your resume should always be accompanied by a cover letter, in which you frame the resume and your candidacy around your unique qualities and express your energy, enthusiasm, and personality – qualities that are difficult to express in a resume. It also should be written with the expectation that a prospective employer will use your resume as the basis for raising several questions about your experience, skills, and accomplishments during job interviews. Therefore, you need to relate the contents of your resume to both the cover letter and the job interview as well as other job search activities, such as research and networking, for which you will be using your resume.

TIP #51
Write your own resume, but seek professional assistance if necessary.

Whether or not you write your own resume depends on how good you are at writing and how much you are willing to spend on hiring a professional. Some people can do it on their own by following the advice and examples found in resume writing books. Others, however, have difficulty being objective about themselves, putting all the elements together, and writing in the language of employers. After all, many of them were taught from childhood not to talk or brag about themselves! While we prefer that you write your own resume because it will more accurately reflect your interests, skills, abilities, and goals, as we noted in Tips #35-39, we recognize that professional help, such as that outlined in Tip #21, is sometimes needed at critical stages of one's job search. If writing a resume is something you have difficulty doing, by all means seek professional help. Paying a professional to put together a winning resume will more than pay for itself if it results in job interviews and offers. A professional resume writer may charge from $100 to $600 to produce a first-class resume. If you are interested in contacting a professional resume writer, you are well advised to explore the resources on these professional resume writing websites:

- **Career Masters Institute**   www.cminstitute.com
- **Professional Association of Resume Writers and Career Coaches**   www,parw.com
- **Professional Resume Writing and Research Association**   www.prwra.com
- **National Resume Writers' Association**   www.nrwa.com

Check out some of these websites which are sponsored by professional resume writers. Most of them will give you a free resume critique prior to using their fee-based services:

- **A and A Resume**   www.aandaresume.com
- **A-Advanced Resume Service**   www.topsecretresumes.com
- **Advanced Career Systems**   www.resumesystems.com
- **Advanced Resume Services**   www.resumeservices.com
- **The Advantage**   www.advantageresume.com
- **Cambridge Resume Service**   www.cambridgeresume.com
- **Career-Resumes**   www.career-resumes.com
- **College-Resumes**   http://college-resumes.com
- **eResumes (Rebecca Smith's)**   www.eresumes.com
- **e-resume.net**   www.e-resume.net
- **Executiveagent.com**   www.executiveagent.com
- **Free-Resume-Tips**   www.free-resume-tips.com
- **Leading Edge Resumes**   www.leadingedgeresumes.com
- **Resume.com**   www.resume.com

- ResumeMaker   www.resumemaker.com
- WSACORP.com   www.wsacorp.com

TIP #52
Craft a resume that represents the real you.

Writing a first-class resume that showcases your major strengths takes more than a few hours to complete. Assuming you have conducted a thorough self-assessment and crafted a targeted objective, developing each section of your resume will take some time. You'll want to draft and re-write each section, conduct both internal and external evaluations (see Tip #107), and write the final version for distribution. This whole process may take a few days or a couple of weeks. Whatever you do, make sure you spend sufficient time to complete each section of your resume. It needs to be perfect in every respect since it will represent your best effort to the reader. It could well lead to a terrific job that pays $20,000, $30,000, or $50,000+ more than you currently make.

TIP #53
Always remember what employers are looking for in candidates.

Many job search and recruitment changes have taken place during the past two decades, especially the role of the Internet. However, some things have remained the same. Take, for example, what employers are looking for in candidates: They want problem-solvers who are focused on their best interests. They are seeking talented individuals who can contribute to the productivity and profitability of their organizations. Always remember this as you write and market your resume. Each section of your employer-centered resume should be focused on the needs of employers.

TIP #54
Be honest but not stupid in what you put on your resume and communicate to prospective employers.

While it's important to be honest in everything you do, honesty does not mean you have to be stupid in what you reveal about yourself to others. You are not required to volunteer red flags or confess sins to employers.

Focus on highlighting your **strengths** rather than revealing yourweak-nesses. After all, employers want to hire your strengths rather than your weaknesses.

TIP #55
People with not-so-hot backgrounds should consult specialized career resources or contact a career professional who is familiar with their special needs and challenges.

If you have red flags in your background, such as job hopping, lack of education, frequent terminations, limited skills, drug or alcohol abuse, physical and/or mental health issues, or a criminal background, that are likely to be revealed during your job search and eventually on the job, you may need specialized advice and professional services aimed at handling your not-so-hot background. Consult our three specialty books, which are designed for people with not-so-hot backgrounds: *Best Resumes and Letters for Ex-Offenders, The Ex-Offender's Job Hunting Guide*, and *Job Interview Tips for People With Not-So-Hot Backgrounds* (Impact Publications). The resume book includes contact information on professional resume writers and career coaches who regularly work with such individuals. Career professionals who work with community-based One-Stop Career Centers (www.careeronestop.org) also frequently work with individuals with not-so-hot backgrounds. Ex-offenders also should consult our specialty website for useful job search tips: www.exoffender reentry.com.

TIP #56
Set aside enough time to produce a first-class resume.

Producing a quality resume is not a slam-dunk exercise. To do it right, you need to set aside sufficient time to gather information on yourself and draft each section of the resume. If you are writing it from scratch, expect to spend up to 40 hours in crafting your resume. Just writing a 25-word job objective may take several days of writing and re-writing until you get it right. When allocating time for your resume, think of your resume as being worth $1 million or more. After all, it may be responsible for acquiring a job that generates more than $1 million of additional income over the next 10 to 20 years. If your next job may be worth that much, it needs a serious investment of your time and effort. This principle of time allocation applies to all other stages of your job search, especially research and networking. One of the major reasons job seekers have difficulty implementing a successful job search is their failure to set aside sufficient time to complete and follow through with their job search. They simply don't take it seriously enough by devoting adequate time for achieving success. If, for example, they spent 40 hours rather than two hours writing their resume, they would most likely produce a first-class resume. If they made 25 rather than two networking contacts a week, they would generate more informational interviews and referrals. Be sure to assess how well you are allocating your time to your job search. If you make this a top priority activity, you may be able to achieve amazing results!

TIP #57
Never start your job search by first writing your resume, but do get started quickly.

As we noted in Tip #2, writing a resume should occur **after** you have completed several other preliminary job search steps. Unfortunately, many job seekers begin their job search by writing their resume. Not knowing what they do well and enjoy doing and lacking a clear objective, they product "obituary" resumes that primarily summarize their work history rather than communicate their strengths and accomplishments to prospective employers. While they will eventually land a job, chances are they will try to fit into a job rather than find one that is fit for them. If you write your resume after completing the necessary foundation job search steps, you should be able to produce a powerful employer-centered resume that clearly communicates your qualifications to employers. Your resume will become the central element for launching a purpose-driven job search. In the end, you'll land a job that's right for you. But don't let lots of time go by before writing your resume. Make it a top priority activity in your job search. Write your resume near the beginning of your job search – make this a thorough two- to three-week job search orientation project. By so doing, you'll force yourself to engage in a series of assessment, research, and networking activities that should result in focusing your search on your interests, skills, abilities, values, and goals. If you do this, your resume will become the driving force around which you organize all other job search activities.

TIP #58
Write your resume early on in your job search
in order to keep yourself focused.

While it's important to complete all preliminary steps before writing your resume, try to complete these other steps as quickly as possible so you can soon produce a preliminary resume with which you can initiate your networking campaign and begin communicating with prospective employers. The sooner you finish your resume, the more focused will be your job search campaign. As indicated in the time line of Tip #3, plan to complete your resume within the first three weeks of your job search.

TIP #59
Consider alternatives to a resume, but make
sure you first write your resume before
completing those other alternatives.

It's fashionable these days to "think outside the box" when looking for a job. Some so-called experts may tell you that it's not necessary to have a resume or that resumes are now obsolete. Don't believe such nonsense, which is usually propagated by individuals who want to sell you some other form of snake oil they are offering to naive job seekers. Resumes are here to stay and in a very big way. They are the central currency of any job search. Since employers want to see your resume before inviting you to a job interview, it's important that you produce a first-class resume that clearly communicates your qualifications to employers. At the same time, you should consider developing other forms of job search communication that further strengthen your candidacy. These include curriculum vitae, portfolios, websites, videos, leadership profiles, executive branding statements, and proposals. Portfolios, which showcase job seekers' accomplishments and present evidence of performance, are often required for certain jobs, especially in the visual arts but also in many other types of jobs. Some of these alternatives to a resume are controversial, especially anything involving video elements that begin encroaching on verbal and nonverbal elements of the job interview. For information on these resume alternatives, see the following books:

Executive Job Search for $100,000 to $1 Million+ Jobs: Resumes, Career Portfolios, Leadership Profiles, Executive Branding Statements, and More, Wendy S. Enelow and Louise M. Kursmark (Impact Publications, 2006)

Create Your Digital Portfolio, Susan Amirian and Eleanor Flanigan (JIST Publishing, 2006)

Career Portfolio Workbook, Frank Satterthwaite and Gary D'Orsi (McGraw-Hill, 2002)

How to Prepare Your Curriculum Vitae, Acy Jackson and Kathleen Geckeis (McGraw-Hill, 2003)

Building Your Career Portfolio, Carol A. Poore (Thomson Delmar Learning, 2001)

TIP #60
Select a format that best showcases your strengths in relationship to the employer's needs.

Resume formats come in several forms. The three major formats are chronological, functional, and hybrid. The **chronological resume**, which lists work history and related accomplishments in reverse chronological order, is preferred by most employers. It's an excellent format for individuals who want to showcase their progressive work experience in a particular career or occupational field. The **functional resume**, which emphasizes key skills rather than specific employment experience, is ideal for individuals with little work experience or who are changing career or occupational fields. People with not-so-hot employment backgrounds, or those who have employment time gaps that would be accentuated if they used a chronological resume format, prefer using these types of resumes. The **hybrid resume** tries to marry the best of both words – emphasize progressive employment experience and skill sets. This type of resume is a good choice for individuals making a career change in a closely related career or occupational field or for those who wish to emphasize their motivated abilities and skills in a separate section for capturing the attention of employers who are looking for patterns of behavior. At least from the perspective of prospective employers, you are best off creating a resume using the chronological or hybrid format.

TIP #61
Avoid functional resumes, unless you lack experience or have something to hide!

While there is a time and place for functional resumes, and they are useful exercises in synthesizing skill sets, as a general rule you should try to avoid such resumes. The reason is very simple: many employers are suspicious of resumes that attempt to downplay evidence of progressive work experience. Such resumes may in and of themselves become red flags – they appear to be written by someone who is trying to hide something, such as the lack of direct work experience, excessive job hopping, jobs in unrelated occupational fields, or lengthy periods of unemployment. If you need to downplay your lack of direct and progressive work experience – you're a graduating student with little work experience, someone who is making a major career change, a job hopper, or an ex-offender – consider developing a functional resume. But also be prepared to explain your lack of progressive employment experience when you get a screening telephone call or are invited to a job interview.

TIP #62
Be cautious of well-meaning resume advice from friends, and even from so-called resume experts.

Many people will freely give you resume and job search advice, whether you ask for it or not! Some may even give you a copy of their resume or recommend that you creatively plagiarize examples of outstanding resumes. Indeed, most people love to give free advice as long it doesn't directly affect them. As you will quickly discover, much of this advice will be contradictory and confusing. If, for example, you listened to some people, they would have you spend most of your time looking for jobs on the Internet, which research shows is not a good use of your time. One thing is for sure: most of this advice will be anecdotal, reflecting the experiences of individuals who probably conducted a less than stellar job search that did not focus on their strengths. After all, anyone can find a job. Finding one you really love takes special effort – something that happens among those who don't listen to all the free and "well-meaning" advice they get from friends.

TIP #63
Avoid common resume errors.

Job seekers repeatedly make numerous resume errors that knock them out of competition. Make sure your resume is not "dead upon arrival," by avoiding their frequently observed resume errors:

1. Not related to the reader's interests or needs
2. Fails to represent the real candidate.
3. Unrelated to the position in question.
4. Too long or too short.
5. Unattractive with a poorly designed format, small type style, and crowded copy.
6. Misspellings, poor grammar, wordiness, and repetition.
7. Punctuation errors.
8. Lengthy phrases, long sentences, and awkward paragraphs.
9. Slick, amateurish, or "gimmicky" – appears over-produced.
10. Boastful, egocentric, and aggressive.
11. Dishonest, untrustworthy, or suspicious information.
12. Missing critical categories, such as experience, skills, and education.
13. Difficult to interpret because of poor organization and lack of focus – uncertain what the person has done or can do.
14. Unexplained time gaps between jobs.
15. Too many jobs in a short period of time – a job hopper with little evidence of career advancement.
16. No evidence of past accomplishments or a pattern of performance from which to predict future performance; primarily focuses on formal duties and responsibilities that came with previous jobs.
17. Lacks credibility and content – includes a great deal of fluff and "canned" resume language.
18. States a strange, unclear, or vague objective.
19. Appears over-qualified or under-qualified for the position.
20. Includes distracting personal information that does not enhance the resume nor the candidate.
21. Fails to include critical contact information (telephone number and e-mail address) and uses an anonymous address (P.O. Box number).

22. Uses jargon and abbreviations unfamiliar to the reader.
23. Embellishes name with formal titles, middle names, and nick-names which make him or her appear odd or strange.
24. Repeatedly refers to "I" and appears self-centered.
25. Includes obvious self-serving references that raise credibility questions.
26. Sloppy, with handwritten corrections – crosses out "married" and writes "single"!
27. Includes red flag information such as being incarcerated, fired, lawsuits or claims, health or performance problems, or stating salary figures, including salary requirements, that may be too high or too low.

Employers also report encountering several of these **production, distribution, and follow-up errors**:

1. Poorly typed and reproduced – hard to read.
2. Produced on odd-sized paper.
3. Printed on poor quality paper or on extremely thin or thick paper.
4. Soiled with coffee stains, fingerprints, or ink marks.
5. Sent to the wrong person or department.
6. Mailed, faxed, or e-mailed to "To Whom It May Concern" or "Dear Sir."
7. E-mailed as an attachment which could have a virus if opened.
8. Enclosed in a tiny envelope that requires the resume to be unfolded and flattened several times.
9. Arrived without proper postage – the employer gets to pay the extra!
10. Sent the resume by the slowest postage rate possible.
11. Envelope double-sealed with tape and is indestructible – nearly impossible to open by conventional means!
12. Back of envelope includes a handwritten note stating that something is missing on the resume, such as a telephone number, e-mail address, or new mailing address.
13. Resume taped to the inside of the envelope, an old European habit practiced by paranoid letter writers. Need to destroy the envelope and perhaps also the resume to get it out of the envelope.

14. Accompanied by extraneous or inappropriate enclosures which were not requested, such as copies of self-serving letters or recommendations, transcripts, or samples of work.

15. Arrived too late for consideration.

16. Came without a cover letter.

17. Cover letter repeated what was on the resume – did not command attention nor move the reader to action.

18. Sent the same or different versions of the resume to the same person as a seemingly clever follow-up method.

19. Follow-up call made too soon – before the resume and letter arrived!

20. Follow-up call was too aggressive or the candidate seemed too "hungry" for the position – appeared needy or greedy.

Since the resume is vitally important to getting a job interview, make sure your resume is error-free. Spend sufficient time crafting a resume that shouts loud and clear that you are someone who should be interviewed for a position.

TIP #64
Write one basic resume from which you can customize other resumes.

Customizing your resume for specific employers doesn't mean you should write different resumes for different audiences. In fact, we've encountered some job seekers who have three different resumes with three different objectives! Not surprisingly, these people also don't know what they want to do and accordingly communicate their lack of goals to employers. Your objective should guide you in customizing various sections of your resume in reference to the needs of specific employers.

TIP #65
If your current resume is more than three years old, consider rewriting it rather than revising it.

Since you and your job change, so too should your resume. Employers look for progressive job experience, patterns of accomplishments, and current skill sets. If your resume is more than three years old, dust it off and seriously consider writing it from scratch. Chances are your old resume was not employer-centered, it lacked a strong objective, and failed to communicate a pattern of accomplishments. You want your new resume to tell a story that will grab the attention of employers who will want to invite you to a job interview – you are a very focused individual with a record of accomplishments. Whoever hires you will get someone who will produce exceptional results.

TIP #66
Write both paper and electronic versions of your resume.

In today's job market, you need both a paper and electronic resume. Despite using resume databases and requesting that resume be transmitted via e-mail, many employers still welcome a paper version of your resume. You will especially need a paper resume when you network for information, advice, and referrals as well as when you interview for a job. At the same time, many employers will ask you to e-mail your resume, and most employment websites will require an electronic version of your resume to be entered into their databases. Start by writing a paper resume which observes all the rules of good design and content. Then convert that basic resume into an electronic version. For information on how to best write an electronic resume, review these four books:

> *Resumes for Dummies*, Joyce Lain Kennedy (John Wiley & Sons)
> *e-Resumes,* Susan Britton Whitcomb and Pat Kendall
>   (McGraw-Hill)
> *e-Resumes*, Pat Criscito (Barron's Educational Services)
> *Electronic Resumes and Online Networking*, Rebecca Smith
>   (Career Press)

Rebecca Smith also operates a website that provides useful online assistance for writing an electronic resume: www.eresumes.com.

TIP #67
Keep your resume to one or two pages, unless your situation justifies going to three or more pages.

The general rule for resume length is one to two pages, depending on your experience. For someone first entering the job market, or with less than five years of work experience, the one-page resume should be fine. If you have a considerable amount of experience, go to a two-page resume. Avoid exceeding two pages since employers generally lose attention after reading one or two pages. At the same time, you may break this one- to two-page rule in certain cases, especially if you are applying for a position within your company, in education, or for an international job. Educators, for example, prefer CVs (curriculum vitae), which can run five to 20 pages and include all types of detailed information on educational activities, from presenting conference papers and publishing articles to chairing committees and receiving research grants. International job seekers often encounter employers who want to see lengthy resumes that include all types of details on international activities; in fact, many of them will reject candidates who present only a one- to two-page resume. They view it as too brief and superficial for their needs. Even some executives may want to go to five-page resumes that detail their specific accomplishments. However, since many executives are recruited through executive recruiters, they will be advised by their recruiter as to the appropriate length of their resume. Electronic resumes can run more than two pages and include a complete work history with a rich selection of keywords.

TIP #68
Select the proper order of categories given your level of experience.

Always follow the principle of putting the most important information first. On a resume this means starting with your name and contact information – mailing address and telephone number and perhaps your fax number, and/or e-mail address. Immediately follow this section with important summary information – "Objective" and "Summary of Qualifications." These three elements make a strong five-second impression – who you are, what you want to do, what you have done, and what major strengths (competencies) you will most likely bring to a new employer.

The ordering of categories depends on your level of experience and the type of resume you select. If you have little or no direct work experience and your educational background appears to be your best qualification, put your education at the very top, just after your contact information and objective. If you have a great deal of experience, put your experience near the top. For most people using a chronological resume, the sequence of categories will be as follows:

1. Contact Information
2. Objective
3. Summary of Qualifications
4. Professional Experience
5. Education
6. Professional Affiliations

Combination and functional resumes will include other categories such as Work History. If you write a scannable resume, a Keyword Summary should replace the Objective and Summary of Qualifications.

TIP #69
Treat education as a potential positive or negative qualification.

Always remember that employers view education as an indicator of skills, accomplishments, and personal qualities. Except in the field of education,

Education usually means knowledge, skills, persistence, connections, and certification.

few employers will hire you because of your educational achievements. Education usually means knowledge, skills, persistence, connections, and certification. For some jobs a high school education with additional training leading to certification is sufficient. For other jobs, the failure to complete a four-year college degree will be a negative. Indeed, if you failed to complete college, your educational experience may be a negative – you're not too bright, you lack persistence and follow-through, and you're not part of an accomplished group. If you highlight your Ph.D. but you're seeking a job that only requires a bachelor's degree, your education will most likely be a negative. Always try to highlight your education as an accomplishment involving both personal qualities and professional skills. If, for example, you are a recent college graduate who achieved a 3.8 grade point average on a 4.0 scale while also working your way through college, highlight those facts in the education section of your resume. If you are currently working on a degree or acquiring some form of education and training, include that information on your resume. It indicates that you are in a learning mode – one of the most important requirements in today's workplace. If you acquired education and training not related to your objective, you may want to deemphasize that experience since it may raise some questions about your goals.

TIP #70
Avoid including potential red flags on your resume that could raise objections to calling you in for a job interview.

Always remember that employers are looking for reasons to eliminate you from further consideration as well as reasons to hire you. Red flags come in many different forms, from obvious resume errors (see Tip #63) to questions about your knowledge, experience, skills, and truthfulness. Red flags can encompass many different things: lack of appropriate education, skills, and experience; over-qualified; excessive number of jobs in a short period of time; obvious time gaps between jobs; an objective unrelated to previous jobs held; salary requirements appearing on resume; drug and alcohol abuse; chronic health problems; bankruptcy; history of arrests and/or incarceration; behavioral problems (dishonesty, anger, abusiveness, violence); and personal issues (divorce, bankruptcy, learning disorder, depression, bipolarism). We examine several of these red flags in _Job Interview Tips for People With Not-So-Hot Backgrounds_ (Impact Publications). While most of us have red flags in our backgrounds (over 50 million America's have been arrested), you should not volunteer any red flags on your resume. Again, your goal is to persuade the reader to invite you to a job interview. The interview is the proper place to address any red flag issues raised by the prospective employer – but not by you!

TIP #71
Avoid accentuating weaknesses on your resume.

Always remember that employers want to hire **strengths** and avoid weaknesses in candidates. Everything you put on your resume should emphasize what it is you do well and enjoy doing in relation to the employer's needs. If, for example, a position requires someone with excellent training and presentation skills, be sure to reveal if you have such skills. Try to quantify your accomplishments related to these skills ("trained 30+ supervisors a month who consistently gave the program a 97 percent excellent to outstanding rating"). Those accomplishments provide evidence to the reader that you have stories that validate your predictable pattern of performance. Therefore, the prospective employer needs to invite you to a job interview in order to hear your stories and discover what it is you will likely do for them.

TIP #72
Be particularly sensitive to including any obvious time gaps on your resume.

Time gaps on a resume are potential red flags that raise questions about your suitability for employment. Many candidates accentuate time gaps by detailing actual stop and start employment months. Remember, employers are always looking for clues to eliminate candidates from further consideration. Candidates who are obsessive about detailed accuracy will often shoot themselves in the foot with information that leads to possible negative speculation. For example, someone who may have been out of work for four to six months might reveal this fact when they detail their inclusive employment dates under their work history:

> February 1997 to March 1999
> September 1999 to December 2002
> May 2003 to June 2006

Presenting employment dates in this manner will probably raise questions about what the candidate was doing between April and August 1999 and between January and April 2003. Was he or she unemployed, incarcerated, ill, or institutionalized? There is no need to include the months of employment. If, instead, the person only listed the inclusive years, no one would question potential time gaps:

> 1997 to 1999
> 1999 to 2002
> 2003 to 2006

If you've been incarcerated for a lengthy period of time, you can deal with your employment time gap a couple of creative ways. First, leave off all employment dates by using a functional resume; organizing your resume chronologically will stress obvious time gaps. Second, if you worked in prison (usually laundry, grounds keeping, and janitorial work), you may want to include the prison as your employer. Stating your prison experience in this form will raise an obvious red flag:

> Pennsylvania State Prison, 2001-2005

It says you're an ex-con who served four years behind bars. This information on a resume greatly diminishes the likelihood of being invited to an interview. Try restating your prison experience in this form, which is equally truthful and free of the obvious red flag:

State of Pennsylvania, 2001-2005

For these and other creative ways to deal with time gaps, see Wendy Enelow's and Ron Krannich's *Best Resumes and Letters for Ex-Offenders* (Impact Publications). Again, the focus of your resume should be on communicating your skills and accomplishments in reference to the employer's needs. When you raise obvious red flags, as in our examples, you distract from the main purpose of your resume. Be very careful how you present everything on your resume. Here's the simple and safe don't-speculate-about-me principle to follow: If you don't have a steady and progressive chronological work history to showcase on your resume, then don't stress that fact by organizing your resume chronologically!

TIP #73
Job hoppers need to rework their experience section to avoid showcasing any obvious red flags.

No one wants to hire an obvious job hopper, unless it's for a job that normally has a high turnover rate and involves limited skills and training, such as a waiter in a restaurant (some restaurants have 80 to 90 percent annual turnover rates) or a construction worker. Job hoppers are often more trouble than they are worth since they are costly employees to train and maintain. If you are an obvious job hopper – change jobs every one to two years – don't accentuate your rather unstable and questionable work history by detailing every job you held. Consider grouping them together and then summarizing your experience in functional terms. Take the following example:

Assistant Manager, Trebles Gourmet: July 2005 to Present
Guest Relations, Fortney's Seafood: February 2004 to March 2005
Assistant Manager, Jake's Lounge: June 2003 to December 2003
Waiter, D&K Restaurant: December 2002 to April 2003
Waiter, Joe's Bar and Grill: June 2002 to September 2002

This candidate obviously has a strong pattern of job hopping – five employers in three years! Would you want to hire this person? Anyone reading this chronology of work history will see an obvious red flag – they will be lucky if this person stays more than six months before moving on again. However, the same work history could be summarized in a more neutral manner that would not accentuate a history of job hopping:

Restaurant operations and management: 2002 to Present

In this example, specific employers are not identified and five different positions are synthesized into "Restaurant operations and management." If invited to a job interview, this candidate will probably have to explain what this means. At that point she can elaborate why she held so many different jobs during a three-year period. For example, she may have been going to school full-time while working in a variety of part-time jobs.

TIP #74
Include jobs for the past 10 years only.

It's not necessary to include all of your jobs, especially if they are dated and show little relationship to your current profession. The rule of thumb is to go back 10 years. Keep in mind that employers want to **predict** your future performance based upon knowledge of your past performance. Include those jobs that best communicate your predictable future performance – skills and achievements during the past 10 years. Include jobs you held 15 or 20 years ago only if they enhance your objective and show progressive career development. Avoid including jobs that appear irrelevant to your objective or may distract the reader from your qualifications. Try to always keep your reader "on message" by focusing on what you want them to most know about your qualifications. This means giving less attention to your history and more attention to your skills and accomplishments. Remember, you want just the right mix of useful information to motivate the reader to invite you to a job interview.

4

Writing Your Own Resume With Impact

ONCE YOU START THE WRITING process, you need to adhere to certain rules for producing a well crafted and targeted resume. The following tips bring together some of the best advice you will find anywhere for writing a first-class high impact resume that is designed to grab the attention of readers who, in turn, will want to invite you to job interviews. If you follow these writing tips, your resume should fit well among the professional examples appearing in Appendix B.

TIP #75
Customize your resume for specific
employers and jobs.

Try to customize your resume as much as possible for particular positions and employers without compromising your stated objective. Avoid writing a resume that looks and sounds like it is mass produced and sent to hundreds of employers. Remember, employers are looking for evidence that they should interview you for **their** position – not for other positions. After carefully examining the position for which you are applying, incorporate the language of the employer in your resume.

TIP #76
Before writing each section of your resume,
develop a database on yourself.

Refer to the various information forms in Appendix A for generating information about yourself: Employment Experience, Military Experience, Community/Civic/Volunteer Experience, Education Data, and Additional Information. Refer to these completed forms as you craft each section of your resume.

TIP #77
Start writing your resume from the bottom
up rather than from the top down.

Here's one of the best tips for getting started in writing each section of a resume. Would you normally start at the top, bottom, or middle? Most people start at the top and that's where they get stuck and frustrated. You may find this whole process will go much faster and will be less frustrating if you start from the bottom and then work up. This strategy focuses on doing the easiest things first – write the factual sections on educational background, professional affiliations, and work history. These sections should go quickly and set the stage for completing the more difficult sections. After doing these sections you can concentrate on the more analytical parts of other sections, such as work experience, statement of qualifications, and your objective. Many resume writers, including the professionals, find the various parts of the resume come together much better if they approach this writing exercise from the bottom up.

TIP #78
The first thing that should appear on your
resume is your complete contact information.

The basic rule for contact information is to make it convenient for the reader to quickly contact you for an interview. Your contact information should include at least the following: name, street address, and telephone number. Decide how formal you want to appear when spelling out and embellishing your name. For example, "Don Perry" sounds more inviting than the more formal and proper "Donald C. Perry, III." Include both landline and cell phone numbers if you may be difficult to reach by landline. You also may want to include your e-mail address and fax number. Use your given name rather than any cute nicknames that could distract from your professionalism. Avoid P.O. Box numbers unless you are truly in transition from one street address to another. Post office box numbers do not enhance your image. Indeed, they may communicate the wrong messages – you appear transient or secretive. Always try to use a street address, unless for some reason it communicates the wrong message (you are unfortunate enough to have an embarrassing street name, such as Big Trouble Lane).

TIP #79
When deciding what to include on your resume, always remember the purpose of your resume – to get an invitation to a job interview.

Don't make the mistake of including lots of extraneous information on your resume, because you mistakenly believe a resume should summarize your history. When in doubt what to include or exclude on your resume, remember the purpose of your resume – to get a job interview. You want to write persuasive ad copy that motivates the reader to take action.

TIP #80
Always include an objective on your resume.

One of the most controversial debates among job seekers and career professionals concerns whether or not to include an objective on your resume. One group argues it's not necessary to include an objective on the resume because (1) it locks you into one type of job, (2) most objectives are trite and thus may diminish your candidacy, and (3) it's best to include an objective in your cover letter. We belong to the second group

An objective becomes the central organizing principle for including other items on your resume.

that argues for **always** including an objective on your resume. Our reasons are quite simple. First, research indicates that employers prefer seeing objectives on resumes. In fact, an objective is considered to be one of the most important things employers look for on a resume! Second, an objective indicates you are a purposeful individual who knows what you want to achieve in the future; employers want to hire such goal-oriented individuals. Third, and perhaps most important of all, an objective becomes the central organizing principle for including other items on the resume; indeed, every element included on the resume should flow directly from the objective. Fourth, an objective stated in the form of skills and outcomes is anything but trite; it's a powerful statement of where you and the employer will be going together in the future. Fifth, a resume without an objective often tends to be disorganized and thus requires readers to interpret what they think the person wants. If an employer has to ask this question after reading your resume, you're in trouble: *What does this person want to do other than land this position and a paycheck?* Don't misunderstand us. People do get interviews with resumes that do not include objectives. In fact, many people get jobs without writing a resume. Our point is that you should always put your best foot forward by creating the very best resume possible. Include an intelligent objective on your resume and you will be communicating your best self to employers. Leave it off your resume and you will diminish your candidacy and force the reader to speculate about what you really want to do in the future.

TIP #81
Avoid putting a trite objective on your resume.

One of the major reasons some resume writing experts oppose putting an objective on a resume is because they have encountered so many trite objectives. Take, for example, these two objectives:

Objective #1

Retail Management position with an opportunity for advancement.

Objective #2

Retail Management position which will use sales/customer service experience and creative abilities for innovative product display and merchandising. Long term goal: Become merchandise manager with corporate-wide responsibilities for product line.

The first one is a typical trite objective that basically says nothing. Worst of all, it's a very self-centered objective – the individual wants a job that enables him or her to get ahead. On the other hand, the second objective stresses key interests and skills as well as focuses on the employer's needs.

The best type of objective is oriented toward skills and results. It follows this format:

> I would like a job where I can use my ability to _____,
> which will result in _____.

For example, at a general level, an objective that follows this format might be stated as follows:

> I would like a job where my experience in retail management,
> supported by strong sales/customer service experience, will result
> in excellent product displays and merchandising.

As noted in our example above (Objective #2), this general objective should be restated on a resume as a job-targeted objective:

> Retail Management position which will use sales/customer service
> experience and creative abilities for innovative product display and
> merchandising. Long term goal: Become merchandise manager with
> corporate-wide responsibilities for product line.

TIP #82
Consider powerful alternatives to, or in addition to, an objective.

While we strongly urge you to include an employer-centered objective on your resume, you may want to consider alternatives to an objective. These include a summary statement, professional profile, summary of qualifications, or keyword summary. Take, for example, these candidates who used a summary or profile to begin their resumes:

SENIOR LEVEL MANAGEMENT/INTERNATIONAL BUSINESS DEVELOPMENT
- *Global Sales & Marketing*   ▪ *Turnaround Leadership*   ▪ *P & L Accountability*

Results-oriented Multinational Business Executive driving innovation by creating and implementing unique market entry strategies. Expert international sales and marketing skills achieving consistent records of aggressive growth in industries with slow buying cycles. Ability to access top officers of targeted companies, recruit in-country sales professionals, create top-performing sales support offices, and establish prominent local brands. Officer/shareholder of travel company and advertising agency. Multilingual in French, English, and German. French citizen with work permits in 15 countries.

ACCOUNTANT
Accounting System Design / Financial Analysis / Personnel Management

Senior accounting professional experienced in financial reporting, cash management, auditing, payroll, benefits administration, and controls for multi-site retail operations. Demonstrated ability to work independently or with teams to reorganize, streamline, and strengthen financial operations to maximize performance and profitability. Core competencies include:

- Strategic & Business Planning
- Internal Financial Controls
- Accounting Policies & Procedures
- Regulatory Compliance
- Computer Systems Management
- Tax Reporting & Preparation
- HR Benefits & Administration
- Multi-Site Operations

These candidates also could have included an objective just before these summary profiles or clearly stated it in a cover letter.

TIP #83
Avoid putting extraneous information on your resume.

Avoid any extraneous information that does not support your objective or communicate your qualifications to employers. Remember, you are not writing your resume to your mother, family, spouse, significant other, or a close friend. This is not an obituary summarizing everything you are or did in the past. The first thing to leave off your resume is the word "Resume"; it's obvious what it is. Avoid including your height, weight, age, sex, religion, health, politics, names and ages of children, spouse's occupation, parent's occupation, and other personal information that is not a bona fide job qualification. We've even come across a resume in which the candidate crossed out "single" and hand wrote "married"! Also, do not include references or salary history/requirements. Apply this simple guiding inclusion/exclusion principle for packing a suitcase: *"When in doubt, throw it out!"* Your focus should be on communicating just enough information about your qualifications so the employer will be interested enough to invite you to a job interview.

TIP #84
Include hobbies and personal statements only
if they strengthen your objective.

Hobbies and personal statements appear as extraneous information on most resumes. However, there are exceptions which would challenge this prohibition. If you have a hobby or a personal statement that can strengthen your objective in relation to the employer's needs, do include it on your resume. For example, if a job calls for someone who is outgoing and energetic, you would not want to include a hobby or personal statement that indicates that you are a very private and sedentary person, such as *"enjoy reading and writing"* or *"collect stamps."* But *"enjoy organizing community fund drives"* and *"compete in the Boston Marathon"* might be very appropriate statements for your resume. Such statements further emphasize the "unique you" in relation to your capabilities, the requirements for the position, and the employer's needs. Again, your resume should be a quick and coherent read for the employer who is trying to screen you in reference to his or her hiring criteria. Personal statements that contribute to such a quick and easy read, and emphasize your unique qualifications, should be included on your resume. They can enhance your candidacy.

TIP #85
Always put the most important information first on your resume.

What you first put on your resume will depend on your level of experience and accomplishments in relationship to the employer's needs. Always follow the principle of putting the most important information first. On a resume this means starting with your name and contact information – mailing address and telephone number and perhaps your fax number, pager number, and/or e-mail address. Immediately follow this section with important summary information – "Objective" and "Summary of Qualifications." These three elements make a strong five-second impression – who you are, what you want to do, what you have done, and what major strengths (competencies) you will most likely bring to a new employer.

TIP #86
Follow the principle of "reverse chronology" when listing any dated items.

Always start with your most recent experience and then work backwards in reverse chronological order. This responds to the expectation of the reader – learning about your most recent relevant experiences. Do not try to compile a complete chronology of your experiences on your resume –

only include positions which you held within the past 10 years. Beyond that only include experiences highly relevant to both your objective and the position in question.

TIP #87
Dates should appear at the end of titles, employers, and descriptions.

Avoid listing dates at the very beginning of your work history or experience sections. The reasoning behind doing this is simple – the most important points you wish to stress are your skills and accomplishments, not your employment dates. Put the dates at the end of each employment description to satisfy the curiosity of employers.

TIP #88
Consider changing a job title to more accurately reflect your previous work.

It's okay to change your job title as long as you do so honestly. Your goal should be to give the employer accurate information on what you have done, can do, and will do in the future. If, for example, your official job title was "Receptionist" but 80 percent of your work was actually in public relations, use a job title that best reflects your work but which is also honest. In this case, you might write:

> *"Public Relations: Developed press releases, contacted media, and arranged interviews with both print and electronic media. Increased the number of media contacts by over 300 percent in the first six months and maintained contact with more than 50 key media contacts each week. Began as a receptionist but job expanded into a public relations position supporting sales and marketing operations."*

Even though your employer did not change your official job title (or your salary!), this description is both accurate and honest as well as demonstrates initiative and progressive career development.

TIP #89
It's okay to exclude certain skills or work history that may make you appear over-qualified for a job.

This is another one of those *"be honest but not stupid"* situations. This issue arises for some people in today's job market who appear over-qualified for what they really would like to do. There is no rule that says you must fully disclose **all** of your work history and education – only what's relevant to the position in question. For example, if you have a law degree but you really want to work as a paralegal, then don't include your law degree on your resume. If you do, you will probably disqualify yourself since you will appear over-qualified for the position and thus "unfit." Your goal should be to get the interview. During the interview you can talk about your legal background and explain why you really want to be a paralegal rather than a lawyer.

TIP #90
Include lots of keywords and action verbs when describing your experiences.

Be succinct and use lots of keywords which consist of action verbs (primarily for conventional resumes) and nouns (primarily for scannable and electronic resumes). Keep your sentences short and to the point. Remember, regardless of whether human readers or electronic scanners process your resume, your document will be skimmed for keywords rather than analyzed word for word, sentence by sentence, and paragraph by paragraph. Like good advertising copy, your resume needs some good headlines to capture and sustain attention.

TIP #91.
Avoid referring to yourself as "I" on your resume.

It's not necessary to directly refer to yourself. If you use action verbs in completing each resume section (directed, supervised, marketed, completed, etc.), the reader assumes you are the subject. Never refer to yourself as "I." Doing so gives your resume a very self-centered tone.

TIP #92
If you lack work experience, include other experiences that can literally "fill in the gaps" and showcase transferable skills.

Take, for example, a student. If you are a student, you can do lots between now and graduation to better position yourself with employers. Your strongest assets appear to be (1) your education, (2) your youth, and (3) your willingness, enthusiasm, and drive to work. Make sure you do a skills assessment and develop a strong employer-oriented objective that communicates both your enthusiasm and willingness to work and learn. Examine your education carefully in terms of skills you've thus far learned and applied. Do a careful analysis of any work experience, be it an internship or volunteer work, to identify your strongest skills and accomplishments. Write a functional or combination resume and include powerful cover letters with each resume you send to employers or others. Be sure to network for information, advice, and referrals, and be persistent in your job search. And between now and graduation, become more entrepreneurial – do some volunteer work or create an internship that best relates to your career goals. Also, don't overlook sales positions, since many are entry-level and require little previous work experience. Your long-term career growth may be dependent on having at one time had sales experience which teaches you to become very entrepreneurial within a company and learn the bottom line – key experience and skills required for today's companies. As many employers will tell you, we are all in sales, whether we like it or not! The sooner you learn this, the better for your long-term career growth.

TIP #93
If you are in the process of changing careers, focus on your transferable skills as they relate to the position in question.

Career changers should avoid chronological resumes because they will stress the fact that you are from a different career field. Use, instead, either a combination (hybrid) or functional resume. These resumes allow you to showcase your transferable skills and accomplishments relevant to your career goals and the employer's position.

TIP #94
Focus on communicating your accomplishments rather than listing duties and responsibilities associated with past jobs.

Since duties and responsibilities come with the job, they say little about what you actually did in terms of **outcomes**. Focus on your **accomplishments** rather than discuss your assigned duties and responsibilities. Your language should incorporate a rich assortment of keywords consisting of action verbs and nouns that clearly communicate your accomplishments to prospective employers. Whenever possible, include statistics and examples that serve as **supports** to indicate how well you performed in previous jobs. Remember, employers are looking for **predictors of future performance**. They want to know what it is you will do for them rather than your unique history. The best predictors of your future performance are clear statements of your skills and accomplishments – what it is you have done, can do, and will do in the future.

TIP #95
Never include salary information on your resume.

Never ever include salary information on your resume – neither salary history nor salary expectations. Salary is something you **negotiate** after you have had a chance to (1) determine the value of the position and (2) demonstrate your value to the employer during the job interview. If you put this information on your resume, you prematurely give the employer the advantage when it comes time to negotiate salary, which is **after** you receive a job offer.

TIP #96
Avoid identifying references on your resume.

Provide a list of references only if requested to do so. Also, take a list of references with you to the job interview where you may be asked for them. And don't forget to inform your references that you are looking for a job and that they might expect to hear from employers soon. Be sure to send them a copy of your resume so they can better stress your positives.

TIP #97
Avoid handwriting any notes or corrections
on your resume.

This may seem to be an obvious tip, but you would be surprised what some candidates have handwritten on their resume – a quick note in lieu of a cover letter or a revision of the facts:

> *"Please consider me for the _____ position. Thanks!*
> *"Will call you next Wednesday to set up an interview.*
> *"I'm exactly what you need."*
> Crossed out *"married"* and handwrote *"single."*
> Crossed out an old address or telephone number.

If your resume needs to be revised, make sure it's a typed revision. If you have something important say about your candidacy, include it in a cover letter. This is not the place to practice time management skills by handwriting notes on a resume!

TIP #98
Be sure to thoroughly proofread your resume.

Many of the errors identified in Tip #63 can be easily avoided by doing a thorough proofreading. As hard and frequently as you may try proofreading your own writing, chances are a spelling, punctuation, or grammatical error will remain. Always have one or two other people proofread for possible errors. Remember, your resume must be error-free or else you will acquire a big red flag for being error-prone.

TIP #99
Your resume should approximate our best examples.

We've included several examples of resumes in Appendix B for your reference. These and many other examples appear in three of our other resume books: *Nail the Resume!, High Impact Resumes and Letters,* and *Military Resumes and Cover Letters* (Impact Publications). Use these examples for guidance, but be sure to write your own resume that reflects your unique goals, experiences, skills, accomplishments, and style. Indeed, you should never "creatively plagiarize" from other examples.

5

Designing, Producing, and Evaluating Your Resume

KNOWING WHAT TO PUT on and what to leave off your resume will take you a long way to producing the perfect document. At the same time, you need to deal with a variety of design and production issues. Many of these issues deal with nonverbal communication – the quality of your design, type font, emphasizing techniques, and paper. Other issues focus on evaluating the quality of your resume.

TIP #100
Choose a layout that is inviting to the reader.

Your resume should have a crisp and clear look that is visually pleasing to the reader. You achieve this by using white space frequently yet sparingly. Avoid the crammed and crowded look; the more blank space you leave around each section, the better. Section headings should be arranged to the left or above each section. Separate each section with at least one and a half spaces – preferably two. Use ellipses to break sentences and ideas on the same line (. . .). You may want to experiment with a variety of different layouts until you achieve the visual effects you desire. The use of single and double lines to accent sections and a full or partial border drawn along the edge of the resume can give it an unusual effect that also looks very professional. Incorporate graphics in your layout if they are appropriate for the position in question.

TIP #101
Use standard emphasizing techniques for paper resumes but avoid them on electronic resumes.

You can emphasize various elements in your resume by arranging space, using different lettering styles and symbols such as bullets (●), boxes (■), hyphens (–), or asterisks (*). You also can CAPITALIZE, underline, and use **bold print** for emphasizing words, phrases, and sentences. However, be careful not to over-emphasize these elements; many readers do not like having their reading flow broken so frequently, and emphasizing too much actually diminishes impact. If you do a good job at editing your resume, you will not need to highlight points so frequently by using such techniques.

On the other hand, when you write an electronic resume, limit the use of such emphasizing techniques since such visuals do not transmit nor scan well. If you've saved your resume in a standard word processing program, you can easily copy it and then paste it into your e-mail program for transmission. However, the end result will not be the same as the original word-processed document because of formatting problems. The person receiving your resume via e-mail will most likely view a garbled document. If an employer asks you to e-mail your resume as an ASCII or plain-text file, you'll need to convert your word-processed resume by doing the following:

- Go to your resume that's saved on your word processing software. Open the file and then save it as an ASCII text, plain-text, or text-only file. Convert your word-processed resume into an ASCII text file using a different name and the file extension *.txt* (for example, *resume.txt*).

- Take out the formatting which would include any special characters or emphasizing techniques not supported by the ASCII character set. This would include boldface, italics, underlining, boxes, bullets, different font sizes, shading, or graphics. You can use characters such as "*" and ">" to substitute for bullets or boxes. Any key you can press on your keyboard, other than function keys, is part of the ASCII character set.

- Capitalize headings for emphasis and left-align each.

- Use a 10-point Courier font; avoid proportional fonts.

- Limit the number of characters to 60 per line.

- Use your "Enter" or "Return" key to break each line rather than let it automatically wrap to the next line.

- Start all text to the left and line-space to different sections rather than use the "Tab" key.

When you're ready to submit your resume via e-mail, paste it into your e-mail program and hit the "Send" button. However, before you transmit it to an employer, it's a good idea to test your composition by e-mailing it to yourself or a friend to see how it looks at the receiving end.

TIP #102
Keep at least a one-inch margin at the top, bottom, and sides.

Avoid creating a crowded and cramped look that accompanies using narrow margins and insufficient white space. A one-inch margin at the top, bottom, and along the sides will give your resume a nice balanced look with sufficient white space along the sides.

TIP #103
Avoid including special borders, graphic elements, or photos on the resume unless they are appropriate for the job in question.

Some candidates get carried away with cute graphic elements that actually work against their best interests. If, for example, you're applying for a position with a bank, don't include floral designs that would be totally inappropriate for such a conservative business. Assume that most employers are like bankers – keep your resume design very basic and conservative. Special graphic effects are likely to distract from your central message. However, if you are in the graphic arts or related art field, you may want to dress up your resume with graphics that demonstrate your creativity and style. Your photo does not belong on a resume. The rule of thumb for photos is this: Regardless of how great you or your mother may think you look in the photo, at least 50 percent of resume recipients will probably dislike your photo – and you. The photo gives them something to pick apart – your hairstyle, smile, eyes, color, dress. Why set yourself up by including a photo that will probably work against you? Your ego is best served with an invitation to an interview based solely on the content of your resume. Focus on your language rather than your photo. This principle is especially important for those who plan to do an online and/or video resume, which we do not recommend since such resumes mix critical face-to-face job interview elements with a resume.

> *Assume that most employers are like conservative bankers – keep your resume design very basic.*

TIP #104
Always type your resume using a standard
word-processing or desktop publishing program.

You're best off word-processing your resume and producing it on a laser printer. Using a computer gives you the flexibility to run as many copies as you wish, as well as customize each resume for individual employers. Computer-generated resumes also are relatively inexpensive. Typewriters are old technology that give you weak production capabilities for producing a first-class resume. Typesetting also is old technology. You need someone who can produce camera-ready copy – a desktop publisher or graphic artist who works in such programs as Microsoft Word, WordPerfect, Adobe InDesign, PageMaker, QuarkXPress, or Ventura. If you don't have a computer, you are well advised to get one and acquire word processing skills. Today's job market requires individuals who are computer literate. If you have someone else generate your resume on a computer, make sure their price includes giving you a copy of the disk. Since you may want to revise your resume later, having it on disk will make the revision process much easier. You may want to use an off-the-shelf resume production program, such as *WinWay Resume, ResumeMaker,* or *Custom Resume Creator.*

TIP #105
Select a very readable typeface.

If you use a word-processing or desktop publishing program, choose serif typefaces (Times Roman, Palatino, Bookman, Perpetua, Arrus, Garamond). Avoid sans serif typefaces (Arial, Humanst, Avant Garde, Verdana) which are more difficult to read. Keep the point size between 10 and 11. Remember, the first thing a reader sees is layout, white space, and type style and size. Your resume should first be pleasing to the eye.

TIP #106
Be sure to produce drafts of your resume
before going into final production.

Produce as many versions of your resume as you need to get it perfect. Keep drafting and re-drafting your resume until it becomes a quick and well focused read. Ask yourself this question: *"In 30 seconds will the employer know exactly what I have done, can do, and will do for him or her?"* If it's not perfectly clear and impressive enough to motivate the employer to invite you to an interview, keep drafting your resume until you get it right. It must have immediate and lasting impact – be a memorable document. Evaluate your resume properly before sending it to your targeted audience.

TIP #107
Don't forget to conduct both internal and external
evaluations of your resume before releasing it
on the street or over the Internet.

You need to conduct two different types of evaluations – internal and external. The internal one involves you assessing various aspects of your resume according to a checklist of evaluation criteria. The external evaluation involves giving your resume to individuals who are competent to assess your resume according to external evaluation criteria. Your best evaluation will come from individuals who are in hiring positions.

An **internal resume evaluation** identifies the strengths and weaknesses of your resume in reference to numerous principles of effective resume writing. Be sure to follow each weak rating with a note to yourself on improving your resume. This activity enables you to evaluate **and** follow through in revising the resume. Refer to the following evaluation criteria to conduct your internal evaluation:

INSTRUCTIONS: Examine your resume writing skills in reference to the following evaluation criteria. Respond to each statement by circling the appropriate number to the right that most accurately describes your resume:

1 = Strongly agree   4 = Disagree

2 = Agree   5 = Strongly disagree

3 = So-so (neutral)

1. Wrote the resume myself – no creative plagiarizing from others' resume examples.   1   2   3   4   5

2. Conducted a thorough self-assessment which became the basis for writing each resume section.   1   2   3   4   5

3. Have a plan of action that relates my resume to other job search activities.   1   2   3   4   5

4. Selected an appropriate resume format that best presents my interests, skills, and experience.   1   2   3   4   5

5. Included all essential information categories in the proper order.   1   2   3   4   5

6. Eliminated all extraneous information unrelated to my objective and employers' needs (date, picture, race, religion, political affiliation, age, sex, height, weight, marital status, health, hobbies) or better saved for discussion in the interview (salary history and references).   1   2   3   4   5

7. Put the most important information first.   1   2   3   4   5

8. Resume is oriented to the future rather than to the past.   1   2   3   4   5

9. Contact information is complete – name, address, phone and fax numbers, e-mail. No P.O. Box numbers or nicknames.   1   2   3   4   5

10. Limited abbreviations to accepted words.   1   2   3   4   5

11. Contact information attractively
    formatted to introduce the resume.   1   2   3   4   5

12. Included a thoughtful employer-oriented
    objective that incorporates both skills and
    benefits/outcomes.   1   2   3   4   5

13. Objective clearly communicates to
    employers what I want to do, can do,
    and will do for them.   1   2   3   4   5

14. Objective is neither too general nor too
    specific.   1   2   3   4   5

15. Objective serves as the central organizing
    element for all other sections of the resume.   1   2   3   4   5

16. Included a powerful "Summary of
    Qualifications" or "Professional Profile"
    section after the "Objective."   1   2   3   4   5

17. Stated work experience in detail,
    emphasizing my skills, abilities, and
    achievements.   1   2   3   4   5

18. Each "Experience" section is short and to
    the point.   1   2   3   4   5

19. Consistently used action verbs and
    the active voice.   1   2   3   4   5

20. Did not refer to myself as "I."   1   2   3   4   5

21. Used specifics – numbers and percentages –
    to highlight my performance.   1   2   3   4   5

22. Included positive quotations about my
    performance from previous employers.   1   2   3   4   5

23. Eliminated any negative references,
    including reasons for leaving.   1   2   3   4   5

24. Does not include names of supervisors or
    others involved with my professional or
    personal life.   1   2   3   4   5

25. Summarized my most recent job and then included other jobs in reverse chronological order.   1 2 3 4 5

26. Descriptions of "Experience" are consistent.   1 2 3 4 5

27. Put the most important skills information first when summarizing "Experience."   1 2 3 4 5

28. No time gaps nor "job hopping" apparent to reader.   1 2 3 4 5

29. Documented "other experience" that might strengthen my objective and decided to either include or exclude it on the resume.   1 2 3 4 5

30. Included complete information on my educational background, including important highlights.   1 2 3 4 5

31. If a recent graduate with little relevant work experience, emphasized educational background more than work experience.   1 2 3 4 5

32. Put education in reverse chronological order and eliminated high school if a college graduate.   1 2 3 4 5

33. Included special education and training relevant to my major interests and skills.   1 2 3 4 5

34. Included professional affiliations and membership relevant to my objective and skills; highlighted any major contributions.   1 2 3 4 5

35. Documented any special skills not included elsewhere on resume and included those that appear relevant to employers' needs.   1 2 3 4 5

36. Included awards or special recognition that further document my skills and achievements.   1 2 3 4 5

37. Weighed pros and cons of including a personal statement on my resume.   1 2 3 4 5

38.	Did not mention salary history or expectations.	1	2	3	4	5
39.	Did not include names, addresses, and phone number of references.	1	2	3	4	5
40.	Included additional information to pique the interest of employers.	1	2	3	4	5
41.	Used a language appropriate for the employer, including terms that associate me with the industry.	1	2	3	4	5
42.	My language is crisp, succinct, expressive, and direct.	1	2	3	4	5
43.	Used highlighting and emphasizing techniques to make the resume most readable.	1	2	3	4	5
44.	Resume has an inviting, uncluttered look, incorporating sufficient white space and using a standard type style and size.	1	2	3	4	5
45.	Kept the design basic and conservative.	1	2	3	4	5
46.	Kept sentences short and succinct.	1	2	3	4	5
47.	Resume runs one or two pages.	1	2	3	4	5

TOTAL [ ]

Add the numbers you circled to the right of each statement to get a cumulative score. If your score is higher than 85, you need to work on improving various aspects of your resume.

You should conduct an **external resume evaluation** by circulating your resume to three or more individuals. For guidelines, give your evaluators the form on page 120. But most important of all, choose people whose opinions are objective, frank, and thoughtful. Do not select friends and relatives who usually flatter you with positive comments. Professional acquaintances or people you don't know personally but whom you admire may be good evaluators. An ideal evaluator has experience in hiring people in your area of job interest. In addition to

External Evaluation

INSTRUCTIONS: Circle the number that best characterizes various aspects of my resume. Please include any recommendations on how I could best improve the resume:

1 = Excellent   2 = Okay   3 = Weak

**Recommendations
for Improvement**

1. Overall appearance	1 2 3		_____
2. Layout	1 2 3		_____
3. Clarity	1 2 3		_____
4. Consistency	1 2 3		_____
5. Readability	1 2 3		_____
6. Language	1 2 3		_____
7. Organization	1 2 3		_____
8. Content/completeness	1 2 3		_____
9. Length	1 2 3		_____
10. Contact information/ header	1 2 3		_____
11. Objective	1 2 3		_____
12. Experience	1 2 3		_____
13. Skills	1 2 3		_____
14. Achievements	1 2 3		_____
15. Education	1 2 3		_____
16. Other information	1 2 3		_____

sharing their experience with you, they may refer you to other individuals who would be interested in your qualifications. If you choose such individuals to critique your resume, ask them for their frank reaction – not what they would politely say to a candidate presenting such a resume. You want the people to role play with you – a potential interview candidate. Ask your evaluators:

> _"If you don't mind, would you look over my resume? Perhaps you could comment on its clarity or make suggestions for improving it?"_

> _"How would you react to this resume if you received it from a candidate? Would it grab your attention and interest you enough to invite the person to an interview?"_

> _"If you were writing this resume, what changes would you make? Any additions, deletions, modifications?"_

Such an evaluation should especially take place in the process of networking and conducting informational interviews.

You will normally receive good cooperation and advice by approaching people in this manner. In addition, you will probably get valuable unsolicited advice on other job search matters, such as job leads, job market information, and employment strategies.

In contrast to the closed and deductive nature of the internal evaluation, the external evaluation should be open-ended and inductive. Avoid preconceived evaluation categories; let the evaluator react to you and your resume as if you were in a job interview situation.

Taken together, the internal and external evaluations should complement each other by providing you with maximum information for revising your draft resume.

TIP #108
Use a standard size paper.

Use standard size 8½ x 11-inch paper. Smaller or larger size papers may set your resume apart from others, but such odd sizes will not enhance your candidacy. In fact, it may not make a lot of difference what size paper you use. In the end, most employers will make judgments based upon the quality of your resume content rather than on paper size or other "dress for success" elements that sometimes candidates confuse with the importance of producing compelling content.

TIP #109
Select good quality paper.

Always try to present your best professional effort when presenting yourself on paper. You can do this in part by printing your resume on good quality bond paper – 20 lb. or heavier (see Tip #113). The paper should have a very professional look and it should feel substantial – just like your candidacy! You'll find lots of good quality paper available at any major office supply store.

TIP #110
Use a good quality printer.

It's best to produce your camera-ready copy (for reproduction) on a letter quality printer, preferably a laser printer. Avoid manual typewriters that produce uneven type and very amateurish documents. Never produce your resume on a dot matrix printer. Most such printers produce poor quality type that communicates a "mass production" quality.

TIP #111
Print your resume on only one side of the paper.

Do not produce a two-sided resume. If your resume runs two pages, print it on two separate pages. Be sure to put your name at the top of the second page, similar to the following header:

Jeff Wilson   Page 2

TIP #112
Do not staple a multiple page resume.

Since your resume may be scanned or copied for other reviewers, do not staple it to a second page or to your cover letter. Staples are very irritating to remove.

TIP #113
Choose white, off-white, ivory, or light gray 20 to 50 lb.
bond paper with 100% cotton fiber ("rag content")

Your choice of paper – color, weight, and texture – does make a difference to resume readers. It says something about your professional style. Choose a poor quality paper and inappropriate color and you communicate the wrong messages to employers. There is nothing magical about ivory or off-white paper. As more and more people use these colors, off-white and ivory colors have probably lost their effectiveness. To be different, try a light grey or basic white. Indeed, white paper gives a nice bright look to what has become essentially a dull-colored process. Stay with black ink or use a dark navy ink for the light grey paper. If you are applying for a creative position, you may decide to use more daring colors to better express your creative style and personality. However, stay away from dark-colored papers. Avoid multi-colored resumes that may not scan well. Resumes should have a light bright look to them. The paper should also match your cover letter and envelope.

TIP #114
Be careful about producing video, multimedia,
and online resumes.

If you are in a creative field, such as film, multimedia, music, art, or theater, you may want to consider producing a video or multimedia resume that simultaneously demonstrates your skills in your particular field. But individuals in other fields should be cautious in using such unconventional resume formats. Keep in mind that most employers are busy people who really don't have the time or equipment to view video or CD-ROM productions – unless they indicate such a resume is acceptable (call and ask if in doubt). Also, video and multimedia resumes introduce elements of a job interview – verbal and nonverbal com-munication – that may be best left to the job interview.

If you do submit a video or multimedia resume, make sure it represents your best professional effort. If you are not talented in these mediums and try to do it yourself on the cheap (just let your video camera roll!), chances are your video or multimedia resume will quickly eliminate you from consideration. Indeed, like putting a picture on a resume, you may not look as good on video as you think you do. You can easily be screened out at this stage by how you look and sound – too young, too old, too heavy, too ugly, too flashy, too slick, too nervous, too funny sounding, too loud, too talkative, too strange, too unenthusiastic. Carefully think through this alternative before investing your time and money in such a production. Better still, if you still consider doing this, "field test" your video production by asking people whose opinions you respect to critique the video from the perspective of an employer.

TIP #115
Consider producing an e-portfolio along with your resume.

More and more job seekers are creating e-portfolios to showcase their professional capabilities. Also known as online portfolios, web portfolios, or digital portfolios, these are essentially stand-alone websites primarily devoted to showcasing an individual's accomplishments. Such portfolios can include a variety of elements for quickly communicating one's qualifications to recruiters and potential employers:

- Resume
- Career success stories
- Goals and philosophy
- Endorsements and testimonials
- Photographs and illustrations
- Audio and video presentations

- PowerPoint presentation
- Sample interview
- Biography
- Professional blog
- Contact information

Information on how to create such online portfolios, along with examples, can be found in the resources identified in Tip #59 (see page 87).

Keep in mind that e-portfolios tend to include a variety of written, audio, photographic, and video elements that can work both for you and against you in getting a job interview. Don't assume they are superior presentations of your qualifications just because they are technically sophisticated and comprehensive. Such online productions may present too much information about you. Always ask yourself this question before investing time and money in creating a digital portfolio: Will it generate more job interviews than a well-crafted and targeted one- or two-page resume? When in doubt about how to best create a digital portfolio, contact a career expert who specializes in developing such presentation tools.

6

Marketing, Distributing, and Following Up Your Resume

MOST RESUME WRITERS focus their primary attention on writing and producing a resume. But once they have the finished product in hand, they fail to market, distribute, and follow up, and thus achieve limited impact. Preoccupied with responding to classified ads or posting their resume online, they neglect some of the most important distribution channels and activities to ensure the success of their resume.

In this chapter we outline some of the most important tips to make sure that your resume has the maximum impact on your job search. In many respects, these are the most important tips related to resumes. For in the end, your resume is only as good as the quality of your marketing, distribution, and follow-up activities.

TIP #116
Clean up any online acts you may be involved with that could raise red flags.

Resumes are not the only things employers look for online related to candidates. Indeed, more and more employers check search engines, blogs, and social networks. Be careful how you appear online! By doing online searches, employers will want to see what else you have written or what has been written about you.

The Internet is literally a two-edged sword – it can work for or against you, depending on the nature of your presence on the Internet. More and more employers "google" candidates' names before inviting them to job interviews in order to acquire additional information that may be beyond the control of the candidate. Such searches may reveal unexpected information about you, such as youthful indiscretions (sex, drugs, and alcohol) displayed on the popular online social networking websites MySpace, Facebook, and Friendster, that could diminish your candidacy.

Some information you can control on the Internet while other information may be beyond your control. If you've already created a personal profile or blog online that is likely to be found when using a search engine, make sure it presents you in the best professional light possible or privatize it with special passwords and access codes. Indeed, you are well advised to enter your name in several search engines to learn what type of presence you already have on the Internet. First impressions count, whether in a face-to-face encounter or on the Internet or telephone. If you have committed some "Internet indiscretions," consider cleaning up your Internet act **before** contacting employers about job opportunities. If not, you may be passed over in silence or asked some embarrassing questions during a job interview concerning what the interviewer learned about you on the Internet.

> *More and more employers "google" candidates' names before inviting them to job interviews. Be careful how you appear online.*

TIP #117
Expect employers to request that you e-mail them a copy of your resume.

In today's job market you will need to transmit an e-mail version of your resume. Make sure you know how to write and distribute a first-class resume that can be e-mailed. Learn to properly e-mail your resume since more and more employers request that resumes be sent to them by e-mail rather than by regular mail or by fax. The principles for producing and distributing (formatting, type style, etiquette, etc.) an e-mailed resume differ from those relevant for a paper resume sent by mail or faxed. As we noted in Tip #101, an e-mail version of your resume must follow certain formatting rules. Do not send it as an attachment since many employers will automatically delete attachments that may have potential viruses. Be sure to select a proper subject or attention line, such as "Resume you requested from Mary Jane Reston."

TIP #118
Plan to target your resume on specific employers.

Broadcasting or "shotgunning" your resume to hundreds of potential employers will give you a false sense of making progress with your job search since you think you are actually making contact with numerous employers. However, you will be disappointed with the results. For every 100 resumes you mail, you will be lucky to get one positive response that leads to a job interview. Indeed, many individuals report no responses after mass mailing hundreds of resumes. It's always best to **target** your resume on specific employers through one or two methods:

- **Respond to vacancy announcements, want ads, or job postings:** Resumes sent in response to job listings also will give you a sense of making progress with your job search. Since competition is likely to be high for advertised positions, your chances of getting a job interview may not be good, although much better than if you broadcasted your resume to hundreds of employers who may not have openings.

- **Target employers with information on your qualifications:** The most effective way of getting job interviews is to network for information, advice, and referrals. You do this by contacting friends, professional associates, acquaintances, and others who might have information on jobs related to your interests and skills. You, in effect, attempt to uncover job vacancies before they become publicized or meet an employment need not yet recognized by employers who may then create a position for you in line with your qualifications. The resume plays an important role in this networking process. In some cases, you will be referred to someone who is interested in seeing your resume; when that happens, send it along with a cover letter and follow up your mailing with a telephone call.

In other cases, you will conduct informational interviews with individuals who can give you advice and referrals relevant to your career interests. You should take your resume to the informational interview and at the very end of your meeting ask your informant to critique your resume. In the process of examining your resume, your informant is likely to give you good feedback for further revising your resume as well as refer you and your resume to others. If you regularly repeat this networking and informational interviewing process, within a few weeks you should begin landing job interviews directly related to the qualifications you outlined in your dynamite resume!

TIP #119
Avoid broadcasting your resume to hundreds of employers or using expensive resume blasting services.

It's always best to target your resume to specific employers whom you know are hiring for specific positions related to your qualifications. The broadcast method gives you a false sense of making progress in the job market because you are sending out many resumes and letters to numerous employers. You'll be lucky to get a one-percent response rate from such junk mailings. However, if you are in a high-demand field, such as information technology or healthcare, have unique skills, demonstrate lots of experience, and make more than $100,000 a year, the broadcast letter may work better for you. You might want to broadcast your resume to two audiences – headhunters and employers.

Several firms specialize in broadcasting resumes primarily to headhunters via e-mail. If you want to try your luck, for anywhere from $19.95 to over $1,000, these resume blasting firms will send your resume to 1,000 to 10,000 headhunters and employers who seek such resumes. While we do not endorse these firms – and we are often skeptical about what appear to be inflated claims of effectiveness – nonetheless, you may want to explore a few of these firms. Many of these firms work on the "dark side" of the job market – sell worthless services to vulnerable job seekers who don't know any better. The firms will tell you they get great results for their clients and they may share a few anecdotes to convince you that their approach works. We're very suspect of such claims, especially anecdotal evidence rather than statistics of the number of individuals who actually got interviews and job offers. This is a broadcast method that we know gets very low results. You'll probably waste your time and money working with such firms. Try this approach: Ask them to structure their fees according to their performance – you only pay them when you get so many interviews and offers. See how they respond to such performance criteria. Chances are they will pitch you the old advertising line – their mailing will "expose" you to several hundred eyeballs. You can easily do this yourself, or hire a $49.95 resume e-mail blaster, and get the same meager results!

TIP #120
The best way to broadcast your resume is to enter it into resume databases, post it on online bulletin boards, or use inexpensive resume blasting services.

We view the resume databases operated by various Internet employment sites as a new form of high-tech resume broadcasting. Resumes in these databases, which can be from 500 to 50,000 in number, are usually accessed by employers who search for candidates who have a particular mix of keywords on their resume. If you have the right combination of skills and experience and know how to write a dynamite resume with language sensitive to the search-and-retrieval software, you should be able to connect with employers through such electronic mediums. At the same time, you may want to use a more traditional direct-mail approach to broadcasting your resume via e-mail – spend from $19.95 to $49.95 on a service to have your resume sent to thousands of employment specialists (primarily headhunters) who request such resumes and to websites with resume databases. Dozens of companies will broadcast your resume for a fee. However, we do not regard these services as effective ways to distribute a resume. At best, they will give you a false sense of making progress with your job search. Some of the major resume blasting firms include:

■ Allen and Associates	www.resumexpress.com
■ CareerXpress.com	www.careerxpress.com
■ E-cv.com	www.e-cv.com
■ Executiveagent.com	www.executiveagent.com
■ HotResumes	www.hotresumes.com
■ Job Search Page	www.jobsearchpage.com
■ ResumeBlaster	www.resumeblaster.com
■ Resume Booster	www.resumebooster.com

- ResumeBroadcaster   www.resumebroadcaster.com
- ResumeHits.com   www.resumehits.com
- ResumeMachine.com   www.resumemachine.com
- Resume Rabbit   www.resumerabbit.com
- ResumeZapper   www.resumezapper.com
- RocketResume   www.rocketresume.com
- See Me Resumes   www.seemeresumes.com
- WSACORP.com   www.wsacorp.com

TIP #121
Post your resume to various employment websites.

Over 25,000 websites in the United States deal with employment. Yes, there's a jungle out there in cyberspace as many job seekers face the daunting task of deciding which sites to visit and possibly use. A good starting point for making such decisions is the AIRS gateway site to job boards:

airsdirectory.com/jobboards

This site includes over 6,500 job boards which are classified by industry, function, occupations, and other useful categories. In the end, however, you'll probably want to concentrate on several of the most popular employment websites and then select a few sites from the AIRS directory that specialize in your occupational field:

- Monster.com   www.monster.com
- Jobcentral   www.jobcentral.com
- America's Job Bank   www.ajb.dni.us
- CareerBuilder   www.careerbuilder.com
- NationJob   www.nationjob.com
- Hot Jobs Yahoo   http://hotjobs.yahoo.com
- Jobs.com   www.jobs.com
- JobSearch   http://jobsearch.monster.com
- CareerJournal   www.careerjournal.com
- CareerFlex   www.careerflex.com
- Employment911.com   www.employment911.com
- EmploymentSpot   www.employmentspot.com
- WorkTree   www.worktree.com
- Job Sniper   www.jobsniper.com

- Vault.com   www.vault.com
- WetFeet.com   www.wetfeet.com
- PlanetRecruit   www.planetrecruit.com
- BestJobsUSA   www.bestjobsusa.com
- Management Recruiters Intl.   www.mrinetwork.com
- Career Shop   www.careershop.com
- NowHiring.com   www.nowhiring.com
- MonsterTrak.com   www.monstertrak.monster.com
- Brass Ring   www.brassring.com
- Career.com   www.career.com
- JobBank USA   www.jobbankusa.com
- Net-Temps   www.net-temps.com
- CareerTV.net   www.careertv.net
- American Preferred Jobs   www.preferredjobs.com
- ProHire   www.prohire.com
- CareerExchange   www.careerexchange.com
- Career Magazine   www.careermag.com
- Employers Online   www.employersonline.com
- EmployMax   www.employmax.com
- EmploymentGuide   www.employmentguide.com
- WantedJobs   www.wantedjobs.com
- RecruitUSA   www.recruitusa.com
- Recruiters Online Network   www.recruitersonline.com
- kForce.com   www.kforce.com
- Dice.com   www.dice.com
- Washington Post   www.washingtonjobs.com/wl/jobs

While you should visit the large employment websites, don't put much hope in their ability to locate a job or employer for you. Large employment websites such as Monster.com, HotJobs.Yahoo.com, and Career Builder.com offer a wealth of information and services to both employers and job seekers. However, these sites are primarily run for the benefit of the paying customers – employers. Job seekers can post their resumes online, browse job postings, and apply for jobs through these sites, but few ever get jobs through these sites. The most valuable aspects of these sites for job seekers are the peripheral services which are designed to keep you coming back again and again (in this online business, you're known as "traffic" when sites set their advertising rates for employers):

- Job Search Tips
- Featured Articles
- Career Experts or Advisors
- Career Tool Kit
- Career Assessment Tests
- Community Forums
- Discussion or Chat Groups
- Message Boards
- Job Alert ("Push") E-mails
- Company Research Centers
- Networking Forums
- Salary Calculators or Wizards
- Resume Management Center
- Resume and Cover Letter Advice
- Multimedia Resume Software
- Job Interview Practice
- Relocation Information
- Reference Check Checkers
- Employment or Career News

- Free E-mail for Privacy
- Success Stories
- Career Newsletter
- Career Events
- Online Job Fairs
- Affiliate Sites
- Career Resources
- Featured Employers
- Polls and Surveys
- Contests
- Online Education and Training
- International Employment
- Talent Auction Centers
- Company Ads (buttons and banners)
- Sponsored Links
- Special Channels for Students, Executives, Freelancers, Military, and others

Huge mega employment sites such as Monster.com include over 80 percent of these add-on services. That site alone is well worth visiting again and again for tips and advice. Most sites, however, only include job postings and resume databases and maybe a newsletter designed to capture e-mail addresses of job seekers who must register in order to receive the newsletter. Again, don't expect too much from these sites in terms of connecting with employers who will invite you to interviews. They have hundreds of thousands of resumes in their databases. Your chances of getting a job interview based on your presence in such databases is not very good. However, you may get lucky given your particular mix of skills and experience. Our advice is to post your resume on many such websites and see what happens. Make sure your resume includes lots of keywords descriptive of your skills and accomplishments, since employers will scan resume databases based upon a keyword search.

You are well advised to focus on smaller specialty websites relevant to your occupation and industry. Many users of Internet employment websites focus most of their attention on a few huge employment sites, such as Monster.com and HotJobs.Yahoo.com. However, they would be better using employment websites that specialize in their industry. For example, if you are an IT professional, your chances of connecting with an employer are much greater on Dice.com and ItCareers.com than on the top

10 mega employment sites. Employers interested in hiring IT professionals are more likely to use these specialty sites than the more general mega employment sites.

Using the Internet in your job search is relatively easy once you have some basic guidance on where to go and what to do. The following books provide details on using the Internet for finding a job. Several of these resources go through the whole process of using the Internet for conducting employment research, posting resumes, and communicating by e-mail. Others primarily annotate the best sites on the Internet:

> *Focus on smaller specialty websites relevant to your occupation and industry.*

> *100 Top Internet Job Sites* (Kristina M. Ackley)
> *Adams Internet Job Search Almanac* (Michelle Roy Kelly, ed.)
> *America's Top Internet Job Sites* (Ron and Caryl Krannich)
> *Career Exploration on the Internet* (Ferguson Publishing)
> *Cyberspace Job Search Kit* (Fred E. Jandt and Mary B. Nemnich)
> *The Directory of Websites for International Jobs* (Ron and Caryl Krannich)
> *The Everything Online Job Search Book* (Steve Graber)
> *The Guide to Internet Job Searching* (Margaret Riley Dikel)
> *Haldane's Best Employment Websites for Professionals* (Bernard Haldane Associates)
> *Job-Hunting on the Internet* (Richard Nelson Bolles)
> *Weddle's Job-Seeker's Guide to Employment Web Sites* (Peter D. Weddle)

See the resources identified in Tip #59 on writing electronic and Internet resumes.

TIP #122
If appropriate, send your resume to
executive recruiters and CEOs.

If you expect to be making $100,000+ a year, chances are you will find over 90 percent of the Internet employment sites irrelevant to your job search. You have very special employment needs that are best met by connecting with headhunters and CEOs rather than surveying job listings and entering your resume in a mega resume database that is primarily accessed by human resources personnel for lower level positions. As we noted in Tip #120, several resume blasting services focus on getting resumes in the hands of such employment brokers. At the same time, a few websites focus on executive-level candidates. They offer databases and networking opportunities that both include and bypass executive recruiters. You should start with the following gateway site to executive recruiters:

www.i-recruit.com

Individuals interested in executive-level positions are well advised to visit the following sites. Several of them charge a monthly or quarterly "membership" fee to access their site while others are free. We recommend starting with the free sites since they may prove to be just as effective as the fee-based sites (we've seen no evidence to the contrary, but you'll have to be the judge). The free sites include:

- 6 Figure Jobs   www.sixfigurejobs.com
- Chief Monster.com   http://my.chief.monster.com
- Management Recruiters Intl.   www.mrinetwork.com
- Recruiters Online Network   www.recruitersonline.com

Major fee-based sites for executive-level job seekers include:

- ExecuNet   www.execunet.com
- ExecutivesOnly   www.executivesonly.com
- Netshare   www.netshare.com

TIP #123
Develop a good record keeping system
for following up your resume.

As you begin applying for many positions and networking for informational interviews, you will need to rely on something more than your memory. A good record-keeping system can help you manage your job search effectively, especially the numerous resumes and letters you have sent. You can do this the old fashioned way by purchasing file folders for your correspondence and notes. Be sure to make copies of all letters you write, since you may need to refer to them over the telephone or before interviews. Record your activities with each employer – letters, resumes, telephone calls, interviews – on a 4 x 6-inch card and file it according to the name of the organization or individual. These files will help you quickly access information and evaluate your job search progress.

If you're computer savvy, you may want to electronically organize your recordkeeping activities using a database program. Check your current software programs for a contact manager, calendar, or tracking/follow-up program. Several software programs are now available for networking and tracking activities. Some, such as *WinWay Resume, ResumeMaker, Sharkware, You're Hired!, Achieving Your Career,* and *Finding and Following Up Job Leads,* are designed specifically for tracking job leads and following up specific job search activities. Many of the large employment websites, such as <u>Monster.com</u>, allow you to manage your resume and track applications online.

One of the simplest and most effective paper and pencil systems consists of recording data on 4 x 6-inch cards. If you respond to classified ads, clip the ad and paste it to the card. Label the card in the upper left-hand corner with a useful reference category and subcategory. For example, in applying for a management trainee position with a food company, your category might appear as follows: MANAGEMENT TRAINEE – food. In the upper right-hand corner, place the name of the company. At the bottom of the card identify the name, title, address, and phone number, and e-mail of your contact. On the reverse side of the same card, record all information pertinent to making contacts for this position. Organize this information by dates and the nature of the contact. Add any information which documents your continuing contacts.

TIP #124
When mailing your resume, send it in a 9 x 12-inch envelope along with a cover letter.

We prefer using a 9 x 12-inch envelope because it keeps your correspondence flat and has greater presence than the No. 10 business envelope. Keep all your stationery matching, including the 9 x 12-inch envelope. If, however, it's difficult to find a matching 9 x 12-inch envelope, go with a white or buff-colored envelope or use a U.S. Postal Service "Priority Mail" envelope.

TIP #125
Type the envelope or mailing label rather
than handwrite the address.

Handwritten addresses look too personal and amateurish, give off mixed messages, and suggest a subtle form of manipulation on your part. This is a dumb thing to do after having enclosed a professional looking resume. Contrary to what many others may tell you, in a job search handwritten addresses – and even handwritten letters or notes – do not gain more attention nor generate more positive responses; they may actually have the opposite effect – label you as being unprofessional or someone who is trying to manipulate the employer with the old handwritten technique. Typed addresses look more professional; they are consistent with the enclosed resume. After all, this is business correspondence, not a social invitation to invite yourself to an interview. Don't confuse communicating your qualifications to employers with selling real estate, automobiles, or insurance – fields that teach salespeople to routinely "personalize" relationships with handwritten addresses and notes to potential customers. Such a sales analogy is inappropriate for your job search.

TIP #126
Send your correspondence by first-class or priority
mail or special next-day services, and use stamps.

If you want to get the recipient's immediate attention, send your correspondence in one of those colorful next-day air service envelopes provided by the U.S. Postal Service, Federal Express, UPS, or other carriers or couriers. However, first-class or priority mail will usually get your correspondence delivered within two to three days. It's best to affix a nice commemorative stamp rather than use a postage meter. A stamp helps personalize your mailing piece and does not raise questions about whose postage meter you used!

TIP #127
Never fax or e-mail your resume unless asked
to do so by your recipient.

It is presumptuous for anyone to fax or e-mail their resume to an employer without express permission to do so. Such faxes are treated as junk mail and e-mails are viewed as spam; they may be seen as an unwarranted invasion of private channels of communication. If asked to fax or e-mail your correspondence, be sure to follow up by mailing a copy of the original and indicating you sent materials by fax or e-mail on a specific date as requested. The poor quality transmission of many fax machines and the bland look of most e-mail will not do justice to the overall visual quality of your resume. You need a paper follow-up which will also remind the individual of your continuing interest in the position.

TIP #128
Send your resume to a specific person rather than to a title or department.

Always try to get the correct name and position of the person who should receive your resume. Unless you are specifically instructed to do so, addressing your correspondence to "Dear Sir," "Director of Personnel," or "To Whom It May Concern" is likely to result in lost correspondence; the mail room may treat it as junk mail. If you later follow up your correspondence with a phone call, you have no one to communicate with. A couple of phone calls should quickly result in the proper name. Just call the switchboard or a receptionist and ask the following:

> *"I need to send some correspondence to the person in charge of _____. Whom might that be? And what is the correct address?"*

Keep in mind that the people who have the power to hire are usually not in the Personnel Office or Human Resources; they tend to be the heads of operating units or hiring managers. So target your resume accordingly!

TIP #129
Don't limit the distribution of your resume only to vacancy announcements.

Your goal should be to get your resume in as many hands as possible. Send it to individuals in your network – your relatives, friends, former colleagues and employers, and anyone else who might be helpful in uncovering job leads. Remember, you want to cast a big net. Let your resume do the fishing by casting it on as many waters as possible.

TIP #130
Be prepared to complete online profile forms
in lieu of a resume.

Many of today's employers operate their own online career centers rather than advertise positions in newspapers or through employment websites. Indeed, you are well advised to visit employers' websites for details on employment opportunities, including vacancy announcements and online applications. Candidates complete online applications which often include a candidate profile form that substitutes for a resume. Much of the information requested for completing this form can be taken directly from your resume. You can clip and paste sections from your resume to complete this form.

TIP #131
Your resume should always be accompanied
by a cover letter.

A resume unaccompanied by a cover letter is a naked resume – like going to a job interview barefooted. The cover letter is very important in relation to the resume. After all, if sent through the mail, the letter is the first thing a hiring official reads before getting to the resume. If the letter is interesting enough, the person proceeds to read the resume. A well-crafted cover letter should complement rather than repeat the content of your resume. It should grab the reader's attention, communicate your purpose, and convince the reader to take action. If you neglect the cover letter, you may effectively kill your resume! In many cases, your cover letter may be more important than your resume in landing an interview and getting the job. Your cover letter should command as much attention as your resume.

TIP #132
Never enclose letters of recommendation, transcripts,
or other information with your resume unless
requested to do so.

Unsolicited letters of recommendation are negatives. Readers know they have been specially produced to impress them and thus they may question your integrity. Like personal photos, unsolicited transcripts may communicate negative messages, unless you have perfect grades. Such information merely distracts from your resume and cover letter. It does not contribute to getting a job interview. It indicates you do not know what you are doing by including such information with your resume and letter.

TIP #133
Attend job fairs with sufficient copies of your resume.

Job fairs are excellent venues for learning about alternative employment opportunities, meeting many employers and marketing your qualifications. As you circulate from one table or booth to another at a job fair, your calling card will be your resume. A good rule of thumb is to bring 25 to 50 copies of your resume to the job fair. Many job fairs also provide copying services, just in case you need to make more copies of your resume. If the employer is interested in you, they will want to see your resume. Best of all, they will give you instant feedback on your qualifications. In many cases, they will interview you on the spot, asking questions you may be unprepared to answer! So make sure you write a terrific resume as well as bring enough copies for every employer you are interested in meeting. Anticipate being asked questions that normally arise during a formal job interview, including *"What are your salary expectations?"*

TIP #134
Follow up your resume within seven days.

Do not let too much time lapse between when you sent your resume and when you contact the resume recipient. Seven days should give the recipient sufficient time to examine your communication and decide on your future status. If a decision has not been made, your follow-up action may help accelerate a decision.

TIP #135
Quickly follow up each resume with
a telephone call or e-mail.

Once you send resumes to prospective employers, be sure to quickly follow up. Don't expect your resume recipient to take the initiative in calling you for an interview. State in your cover letter that you will call the recipient at a particular time to discuss your resume. For example,

> I will call your office on the morning of March 17 to see if a meeting can be scheduled at a convenient time.

And be sure you indeed follow up with a phone call at the designated time. If the employer has received many resumes during this time period, your telephone call or e-mail will remind him or her who you are and your interest in the position. We prefer using the phone for doing this follow-up. A phone call also may give the employer an opportunity to conduct a telephone screening interview. Don't be too pushy at this stage. Use a low-key professional approach. Assuming you are able to get through to the person who received your resume, ask about your resume and the position:

> Hi, this is Emily Orlando. I'm calling in reference to my resume which I sent to you on June 3rd.
>
> Did you receive it?
>
> I know you're busy, but did you have a chance to review it yet?
>
> Do you have any questions at this time?
>
> As I mentioned in my cover letter, I'm very much interested in this position, especially given my recent work at Rogers and Associates which focused on developing a new financial planning program for college graduates. I would love to have an opportunity to meet with you to discuss my work and how my experience might best contribute to your new programs designed for college students. Could we meet soon?

Notice how this conversation line moves from a polite *"Did you receive my resume?"* question to stressing the individual's key strength in reference to the employer's hiring need. Most important of all, this individual closes this follow-up call with an action statement – a request to interview for the job. While this is a moderately assertive approach, it is very targeted and professional. Although the employer may not wish to interview this individual right now, he or she may remember the candidate, re-read her resume, and put her at the top of the interview list. Being **remembered and prioritized** are two of the most desirable outcomes of such a resume follow-up call.

If you have difficulty contacting the individual, try three times to get through. After the third try, leave a message as well as write a letter – paper or e-mail – as an alternative to the telephone follow-up. In this letter, inquire about the status of your resume, mention your continued interest in the position, and thank the individual for his or her consideration.

TIP #136
Follow up your follow-up with a nice thank-you letter.

Regardless of the outcome of your follow-up phone call, send a nice thank-you letter based upon your conversation. You thank the letter recipient for taking the time to speak with you and reiterate your interest in the position. While some career counselors recommend sending a handwritten thank-you note to personalize communication between you and the employer, we caution against doing so. Remember, you are engaged in a business transaction rather than in social communications. We feel a handwritten letter is inappropriate for such situations. Such a letter should be produced in a typed form and follow the principles of good business correspondence. You can be warm and friendly in what you say. The business letter form keeps you on stage – you are putting your best business foot forward.

7

Completing Effective Applications

EXPECT TO ENCOUNTER many jobs that require a job application in lieu of, or in addition to, a resume. While applications used to be primarily used for screening candidates for blue collar and low-paying white collar positions, they are now being required for screening all types of candidates.

Many employers require candidates to fill out job applications. If, for example, you walk into a grocery store or retail business, you may be asked to go to a computer screen, or kiosk, to complete an online application, or you will be given a two- to four-page application form to be completed by hand. Many companies routinely give anyone interested in a job a chance to fill out an application.

As the recruitment process increasingly moves to the Internet, more and more employers require applicants to complete an online profile or mini resume which, in effect, is an application form that can be easily imported into a company's database. Employers prefer using such profiles because they standardize the information received from candidates and make it much easier to assess qualifications.

But completing a job application or online profile is by no means a simple fill-in-the-blanks writing or typing exercise. You need a strategy.

Like writing resumes and letters, you should carefully assess each section, select appropriate language, and be as truthful and forthcoming as possible without being stupid.

The following tips should help you complete a job application to the expectations of employers and improve your chances of getting a job interview.

TIP #137
Prepare to complete each section of
a job application.

You are expected to complete each section of a job application and respond to each question. Unless you have serious red flags in your background, avoid leaving blanks, since no response may raise red flags in the eyes of the employer – you lack attention to detail or you may be hiding something. If you decide not to respond to a question because it doesn't pertain to your situation, write "N/A" (not applicable). If you do not wish to respond in detail to a question because your response may be misin-

> *Avoid leaving blanks, since no response may raise red flags in the eyes of the employer.*

terpreted and thus raise red flags, include a short statement, such as "Will discuss at the appropriate time" or "Please contact for details" or just leave it blank. However, an application that includes blanks leaves the reader to wonder "Why didn't he respond to this question? Is there some problem here?" But if you do write something, the content of what you say may be worse than leaving it bank. It's your call what to do in this situation.

TIP #138
Answer all questions as completely as possible.

Too often job seekers think the purpose of an application is to document their employment history, provide information on salary history, and include a list of references. Yes and no. The person reviewing your application has many concerns that go far beyond a historical record of employment. The individual is primarily trying to screen you out of consideration. The art of handling job applications includes reading between the lines by looking for skills, interests, and anything negative that could knock you out of the competition. Indeed, like resumes, applications can expose possible red flags – you admit to a criminal conviction, you reveal being fired, you have little experience, your previous jobs do not relate to the position in question, your salary history or requirements are too high or too low, you include a strange mix of references that do not relate to previous employment. Given the space available, try to provide as much positive information about yourself as possible. When asked about your employment history, include the employer's name, your job title, inclusive employment dates, and a brief statement of your accomplishments, similar to what would normally appear on an outstanding resume. However, be careful in providing too much information that may distract from your central qualifications, such as any negative reasons why you left previous positions. Always keep in mind the central purpose of completing an application – to get an invitation to a job interview. Like a resume, your application should become an advertisement to interview you for a job. Be complete, but provide just enough information to persuade the reader to contact you for an interview. It's important to respond to each question – no blanks left that could raise questions in the mind of the reviewer about your willingness to disclose. For example, if you don't have a permanent address or telephone number, use the address and number of a friend or relative who agrees to serve as your contact location. Do not appear homeless on an application – it raises all kinds of questions about transportation, stability, and work history. If a question does not relate to your situation, such as military service, type or write "N/A," which means "Not Applicable."

TIP #139
Dress neatly for the application site.

Assume that you will be observed when you complete the application. The person taking your application may make a note about your appearance and communication skills. Since you may end up being interviewed on the spot, dress as if you were going to a job interview and observe all the rules for positive verbal and nonverbal behavior. First impressions are always important, be it on an application, over the telephone, or in person.

TIP #140
Take two copies of the application form.

If you are picking up an application form to take with you, get two copies. Use the one copy to draft your answers and the other copy to submit as a neat, clean, and error-free application.

TIP #141
Read the instructions carefully and follow them completely.

An application is your first screening test in more ways than you may think. Start by reading through the whole application to see exactly what information is required for completion. If you lack sufficient information, don't complete the application since you will be submitting an incomplete application, which is a negative. Return later with the information that you didn't have the first time. Follow the instructions. If it says print, then you print. If it says last name first, then write accordingly. If it asks for a phone number, provide one. If it asks for your supervisor's name, reason for leaving each job, and pay rates, supply this information. If it says provide three references, then give the details on three references. Failure to complete an application according to instructions communicates a terrible message – you simply can't follow instructions, or you have something to hide! No one wants to hire such people. You've just wasted your time filling out an incomplete application.

TIP #142
Use a black ink pen when writing.

Avoid using a pencil or an ink color other than black. In fact, many applications will ask you to use a black pen. An application completed in pencil looks unprofessional and one completed in a non-black ink may be difficult to read if the application is run through a copy machine or scanned into a database.

TIP #143
Try to write as neatly as possible.

The neatness and style of your handwriting may be interpreted by the reader as an indication of your personality and work habits. If it looks sloppy, with letters or words crossed out, the reader may think you are confused, careless, or sloppy in your work habits.

TIP #144
Be prepared to complete each section
of the application.

If you know you will be applying for a job, take to the application center all information you may need to complete the application in full. You may want to complete a mock or draft application form, which you always take with you, that contains most information you are likely to be asked on an application. This would include a list of previous employers, addresses, telephone numbers, employment dates, information about your work, and documents (Social Security number and driver's license). You also want to have with you details on your educational background and references. Trying to recall this information by memory may lead to inaccurate statements or an incomplete application; you'll be demonstrating two negatives to the employer even before the job interview – you are unprepared and you're not serious about employment.

TIP #145
Include all previous employers.

Reveal all of your previous employers, even if you were fired. Many people get fired and it's not held against them by other employers. You can always explain the situation, but you will have greater difficulty trying to explain a major employment gap. If you are an ex-offender, include your prison work experience at a state or federal job, such as Custodian, State of Louisiana, or Machine Operator, State of Texas. If, indeed, you have janitorial duties and operated machines, such as those in the laundry room, these are truthful employment statements that do not prematurely raise a red flag that you served time in XYZ Penitentiary. You have work experience, you used skills, and you have someone who can serve as a reference. Most important of all, you filled in a potential time gap that might have indicated you were hiding something or you were unemployed for a long period of time. Hiding your record indicates you may be a con artist. No one wants to hire someone who is deceptive. If you can't be trusted with the truth at the application stage, why would anyone want to trust you on the job?

TIP #146
If you lack work experience, be creative in revealing your key abilities and transferable skills.

Each year millions of people first enter the job market without formal work experience or a job. However, that doesn't mean they lack work-related experience. If you did not hold a regular job but have volunteer or other life experiences related to skills found in the workplace, include these in the work experience section. Did you assist a group (church, school, sports team, community organization), did you sell something?

TIP #147
Appear educated, even if you lack formal credentials.

Let's face it. Few employers want to hire someone without a high school education. If you lack a high school education but have a GED, include the date you completed your GED. If you do not have a GED, get enrolled in a program **before** you fill out any applications and then state on your application that you are completing your GED in a specific month and year. If you've completed a training program or acquired specialized skills, include those on your application under Education. Make sure you appear educated and thoughtful – no misspelling, poor grammar, or stupid and smart aleck statements – in each section of your application.

TIP #148
Select your references carefully.

Since employers increasingly check references, be sure to include a set of references that is very supportive of your candidacy. Most of your references should relate to your previous employment. They should be able to tell a prospective employer that you have the skills, abilities, and energy to do the job and give examples of your accomplishments and how you work with others. You need to do two things in regards to references. First, prepare your references for your job search by contacting them ahead of time. Inform them of your employment interests and ask if they would be willing to give you a positive recommendation. If you have a resume, send them a copy so they will remember who you are in terms of education, employment, interests, and skills. Second, select a combination of both personal and professional references. One individual should be able to vouch for your character and personality. This person could be a previous teacher, a minister, or a colleague. Avoid including self-serving references, such as a relative or close friend. You don't want a reference checker to call such individuals and ask about their relationships to you and discover they are your parent, uncle, or your close classmate. Such individuals do not add value to your candidacy. Third, type out your list of references, including name, address, telephone number, and e-mail. Take that list with you to the place where you will be completing the application. You don't want to be caught off guard and not have this information when asked to fill out an application.

> *Most references should relate to your previous employment. Avoid including self-serving references, such as a relative or friend.*

TIP #149
Handle sensitive red flag questions
honestly and tactfully.

Two sections on most applications require sensitivity and discretion on your part since your answers could raise red flags that would knock you out of further consideration. First, consider how you would respond to the question if you have ever been convicted of a crime. Indeed, if you are an ex-offender, your need to properly address one of the most sensitive questions on an application: *"Have you ever been convicted of a crime? If yes, please explain."* Most applicants believe they have three choices in responding to this question: Lie, tell the truth, or leave it blank. All three choices may have negative consequences for getting the job interview or keeping the job. In addition, the law may require you to disclose your criminal record to employers, and you must sign the applications, indicating your answers are truthful. However, there is a fourth choice in answering this question which leaves the door open: simply write *"Please discuss with me"* or *"Will discuss at the interview."* These statements indicate you have a conviction, you're not hiding it, and you are prepared to discuss it at the appropriate time. If you must include some details, keep them short and focused on the future, such as *"Will complete parole or probation in 20__."* Depending on the nature of your crime, you cannot adequately explain your record in one or two sentences. Indeed, most short statements raise more negative questions than they answer. This question is best dealt with in a face-to-face meeting where you will have a chance to explain and demonstrate six things – (1) you made a serious mistake, (2) you took responsibility, (3) you've done several things to change your life, (4) you're not a risk, (5) you want a chance to prove yourself, and (6) you are positive, enthusiastic, energetic, and ready to perform beyond the employer's expectations. A similar response should be given to another sensitive question: *"Have you ever been fired?"* Respond by writing *"Please see me"* or *"Will discuss at the interview."* Whatever you do, don't lie; your red flag will most likely show up on a background check and will be legitimate grounds for firing.

Second, if asked about your employment history and reasons for leaving, be careful what you say, especially if you were fired or unhappy with your employer. Candor in this situation can work against you, especially if you use the word "fired" or "terminated." Either leave this section blank or use the universal career transition phrases "sought new opportunities" or "career advancement," which indeed you did.

TIP #150
Minimize abbreviations.

Not all readers share the same knowledge of abbreviations. You can abbreviate the obvious, such as Street (St.), Avenue (Ave.), or Boulevard (Blvd.), but spell out the not-so-obvious. If, for example, you lived or worked in Los Angeles, your application should say Los Angeles rather than L.A.

TIP #151
Avoid vague statements.

Employers look for details that indicate a candidate's qualifications and level of performance. If, for example, you state that you can operate a computer, indicate at what level and with which programs. If you are a driver, indicate what type of vehicle or equipment you work with. The more details you give, the more impressive will be your application and the more confident the employer will be about your capabilities to perform in his or her organization.

TIP #152
Avoid revealing salary information.

If asked to state your salary history or salary requirements, be very careful how you answer this question. In the case of salary history, state a range that would include your base salary plus other compensation, which can run an additional 40 percent over your base salary. For example, if you received a $40,000 base salary on your last job, you may learn you also received an additional $20,000 in benefits. Therefore, your salary history in this case could be stated as $40,000 - $60,000. In the case of salary expectations, you may want to immediately screen yourself in or out by stating a figure. However, if you want to stay in the running it's best to give a salary range rather than a specific figure. Better still, write "Negotiable," since salary is something you want to negotiate. In fact, you need to learn more about the position and the employer needs to learn more about you before you can discuss salary. If you state a figure or even a range at this stage, you begin to reveal your hand. The employer knows exactly where you are coming from in terms of salary expectations. If you are too high, you'll be immediately knocked out of consideration for a job interview. If you are too low, you may not have much value in the eyes of the employer.

If the application asks for your salary expectations (pay or salary desired), state *"Open"* or *"Will discuss at the interview."* Always keep this question to the very end of the interview – **after** you have been offered the job. The old poker saying that *"He who reveals his hand first is at a disadvantage"* is very true in the job search. Get the employer to first reveal his hand before you talk about your salary expectations. You need to persuade the employer to reveal his hand first by letting you know what he normally pays someone with your qualifications.

TIP #153
Include interests and hobbies relevant to the job.

If asked about any interests and hobbies, try to select examples relevant to the job. If, for example, you are applying for an outdoor job that requires physical stamina, outdoor sports interests would be supportive of such a job.

TIP #154
Add additional comments if appropriate.

Some applications will have a section for additional comments. This is the place you want to indicate your goals, state your interests, and make a pitch for the job. Get yourself set up for the job interview by stating something to this effect:

> "I'm especially interested in this job, because I love working with inventory management software and streamlining operations that save companies both time and money. I would appreciate an opportunity to discuss how my experience can best meet your needs."

TIP #155
Remember to sign the application.

The very last thing you need to do is sign and date your application. Failure to do so may invalidate your application and raise questions about your ability to follow instructions.

TIP #156
Read and re-read your answers.

Make sure you proofread your application for any errors, omissions, or misspellings. Like the perfect resume, you want an error-proof application. If you make a mistake and need to rewrite a section, start over with a clean copy of the application rather than cross out any errors.

TIP #157
Attach an achievement-oriented resume
if appropriate.

At least for employers, applications are a necessary evil in the screening and hiring processes. Most applications follow a similar and rather dull format that yields little information about who you really are and what you have done, can do, and will do in the future. Few applications allow the flexibility to state your goals, skills, and accomplishments.

If you write an achievement-oriented resume, submit it along with your application. With a resume, you structure the reader's thinking around your major strengths rather than allow the reader to control information about you, which is exactly what an application does for the employer. If you have developed an achievement-oriented resume that includes your objective and stresses your skills and accomplishments, do attach it to your application. Two of the most powerful sections on your resume – objective and accomplishments – normally do not appear on an application. When you attach such a resume to your application, you should be able to greatly enhance your qualifications in the eyes of employers. Your resume gives your application added value and places you at an advantage compared to other applicants. Your resume, not your application, becomes the central focus of the job interview.

TIP #158
Ask about the selection process and hiring decision.

Once you complete your application and give it to the employer, be sure to ask about the selection process. When, for example, do they expect to start interviewing candidates and making a hiring decision? Would it be okay for you to check back with the employer on the status of your application? When you ask these questions, you open the door to conducting a critical follow-up.

TIP #159
Follow up your application with a telephone call.

Be sure to follow up your application with a telephone call. You should do this within five days of submitting your application. When you call, your conversation should go something like this:

> Hi, this is James Olsen. Last week I submitted my application for the inventory management position. I'm calling to see if you have any questions as well as inquire if we could meet to discuss how my skills and experience can best meet your needs. Would it possible to set up an interview next week?

While this follow-up call may seem somewhat aggressive, keep in mind three things related to your phone call. First, you may be competing with dozens of applicants who do not make such a follow- up call. As a result, you stand out from the crowd, which is something you want to do.

Second, your call indicates both initiative and interest in the job; many employers appreciate encountering such candidates. Third, you have nothing to lose and everything to gain by asking for an interview. If the response is that they will call if they wish to interview you, then ask when you might hear from them and when they expect to make a hiring decision. Try to get as much information as possible on the hiring process. Always end the conversation by indicating your continuing interest in the position and thanking them for the opportunity to apply for the position. Get the person's name and follow up with a thank-you letter which indicates your continuing interest in the position and expressing your thanks for the information and their consideration. Such a thank-you note communicates one of the most important values in the hiring process – you are truly interested in the position and you are a very thoughtful individual. Employers like to hire such people.

This critical follow-up telephone call often results in a job interview. After all, the employer may still be reviewing applications, and your call may force him or her to take a second look at your application (and attached resume).

8

Effective Cover and Job Search Letters

S MANY JOB SEEKERS QUICKLY discover, their cover letters and other types of job search letters are often more important to getting a job interview and offer than their resume or application. Indeed, many employers report it was the cover or thank-you letter that made the difference in selecting candidates. In fact, many job seekers have been hired on the basis of their letters rather than their resume or application.

Don't under-estimate the power of a letter. Too many job seekers primarily focus on the content of their resume to the exclusion of letters. Some of them treat letters as a necessary nuisance and thus produce canned or uninspired letters that diminish their candidacy. Don't let this happen to you. Be sure to pay particular attention to a whole series of letters that need to be written at various stages of your job search. These letters can make a big difference between being accepted or rejected for a job interview and offer.

The following tips and examples in Appendix C introduce you to some of the most important written job search communication. If you follow these tips and examples, you should be able to energize your job search as you express your unique personality and values to employers.

154

TIP #160
Include a powerful cover letter with your resume.

If you want your resume to be "dead upon arrival," just send it without a cover letter or write a short note at the top of your resume, such as *"Please consider me for a position with your company."* Here's the problem: if you are too lazy to craft a thoughtful cover letter, you're also too thoughtless to be considered for a job. Cover letters are an important part of job search etiquette. Employers expect to receive them. They want candidates to communicate information about themselves that is not included in the resume, such as their personality, enthusiasm, and competence. If you view your cover letter as being potentially more important than your resume in getting a job interview, you just might spend a great deal of time crafting a very thoughtful and powerful cover letter.

> *If you are too lazy to craft a thoughtful cover letter, you're also too thoughtless to be considered for a job.*

TIP #161
Write a variety of job search letters appropriate for different job search situations.

Cover letters, which accompany resumes, are only one of several types of letters you need to write during your job search. Other important job search letters include:

- Resume letters
- Approach letters
- Thank-you letters

Some of the most powerful job search letters you can write are thank-you letters. These letters are usually remembered by employers because few candidates are thoughtful enough to send such letters. Different types of thank-you letters should be written on various job search occasions:

- Post-job interview
- After an informational interview
- Responding to a rejection

- Withdrawing from consideration
- Accepting a job offer
- Terminating employment

These are some of the most neglected yet most important written communications in any job search. If you write these letters, your job search may take you much further than you expected.' Indeed, you may be surprised by the positive responses to your candidacy! Numerous examples of these types of job search letters can be found in Appendix C as well as in Ron and Caryl Krannich's *201 Dynamite Job Search Letters* and *Nail the Cover Letter!* and Wendy S. Enelow's *Best Cover Letters for $100,000+ Jobs* (Impact Publications).

TIP #162
Avoid 16 common letter writing errors.

Individuals who receive hundreds of letters from job seekers report similar problems with most letters they read. These problems can be corrected by following a few simple organization and content rules. Letters that don't pass the five to ten second test tend to include several of these errors:

1. **Looks unprofessional in form, structure, and design:** Many letters neglect the basic rules of form, structure, and design. They look amateurish rather than reflect the professional competence of the writer. They simply don't demonstrate the writer's best professional effort.

2. **Addressed to the wrong person or sent to the wrong place.** Many letter writers still forget to include proper contact information or send their letters to the wrong people and places. Make sure your letter includes a complete return address and a telephone number where you can be reached during the day. Also, closely check the name and address of the person who will receive your letter.

3. **Does not relate to the reader's knowledge, interests, work, or needs.** Many letter writers fail to research the needs of their audience and target them accordingly. They simply waste employers' valuable time. If you respond to an ad or

vacancy announcement, make sure you address the requirements specified for submitting your letter and resume.

4. **Includes spelling, grammatical, and punctuation errors.** The worst mistakes you can make in a letter are spelling, grammatical, or punctuation errors. These are unforgiving errors that clearly communicate your incompetence. Such mistakes demonstrate you are either careless or semi-illiterate – both deadly to a job search!

5. **Uses awkward language and the passive voice.** Carefully watch your use of language and try to mainly use the active voice. The active voice gives your writing more energy. Good, crisp, interesting, and pleasing language is something few readers experience in reading letters.

6. **Overly aggressive, assertive, boastful, hyped, and obnoxious in tone.** Employers receive many letters from individuals who try to impress them with what is essentially obnoxious language. They think that telling an employer they are the "hottest thing since sliced bread" will get them an interview. These letters even appear in some books that claim they are examples of "outstanding letters"! We have yet to encounter employers who are impressed by such letters. They tend to be low class letters that follow the principles of low class advertising.

7. **Self-centered rather than job or employer-centered.** Too many job applicants still focus on what they want **from** employers (position, salary, benefits) rather than what they can do **for** employers (be productive, solve problems, contribute to organization, give benefits). Make sure your letters are oriented toward employers' needs. Tell them about the **benefits** you will give them. If you start referring to "you" rather than "I" in your letters, you will force yourself to be more employer-centered.

8. **Poorly organized, difficult to follow, or wanders aimlessly.** Many letter writers still fail to plan the logic, sequence,

and flow of their letters. They often begin with one idea, wander off to another idea, continue on to yet another disconnected idea, and then end the letter abruptly with no regard for transitions. Readers often must examine the letter two or three times to figure out what the writer wants. Such poor writing is inexcusable. You must present yourself in an organized and coherent manner, if you want to be a serious contender for the job.

9. **Unclear what they are writing about or what they want.** Is there a goal or purpose to this letter? Many letters still lack a clear purpose or goal. They assume the reader will somehow figure out what they are writing about! Make sure your letter has a clear purpose. This should be revealed in the first paragraph.

10. **Says little about the individual's interests, skills, accomplishments, or what they expect to achieve in the future.** Your job search letters should tell letter recipients what it is you can do for them. Unfortunately, many letter writers fail to communicate their strengths and benefits to potential employers.

11. **Fails to include adequate contact information.** Be sure to include your complete address, including zip code, and a daytime telephone number. Do not use a P.O. Box number.

12. **Dull, boring, and uninspired.** Employers are looking for individuals who have enthusiasm, energy, and fire. However, most letters they receive give little indication of these critical characteristics. Try to use language that expresses your enthusiasm, energy, and fire. At least start with the active voice!

13. **Too long.** Busy people don't have time to read long letters. Chances are you can say just as much, and more effectively, in a short letter. Follow the principle of "less is best."

14. **Poorly typed.** We still receive letters from people who make typing errors. Word-processed letters often lack basic formatting, such as margins and centering; many are top heavy with the text

occupying the first three inches of the page. The result is an amateurish looking letter that reflects poorly on the professional style and competence of the letter writer. If you write a job search letter, make sure it reflects your **best** professional effort.

15. **Produced on cheap and unattractive paper.** Professional correspondence should be produced on good quality paper. However, many letter writers cut corners and go with poor quality paper. Don't be cheap. Good quality paper only costs a few cents more than the cheap product, and it's easy to find at your local stationery or print shop. It more than pays for itself.

16. **Lacks information on appropriate follow-up actions.** In addition to indicating the writer's purpose, the letter should include information on what actions should or will be taken next. This information normally appears in the last paragraph.

In other words, many letters are just poorly written; they make poor impressions on readers. Letters that avoid these errors tend to be read and responded to. Make sure your letters are free of such errors!

TIP #163
Job search letters should follow four key principles of good advertising.

Several principles of effective advertising can be adapted to business writing and the job search. Indeed, the advertising analogy is most appropriate for a job search since both deal with how to best communicate benefits to potential buyers and users. These principles should assist you in developing your creative capacity to get what you want through letter writing.

Job search letters should be written according to the key principles of good advertising copy. They should include the following principles:

1. **Catch the reader's attention:** While advertising copy primarily captures attention through a visual (headline, photo, illustration), a job search letter can do the same. It should project an overall quality appearance and an opening sentence or paragraph that immediately grabs the reader's attention. Like

any good presentation, an attention-grabbing opening can be a question, startling statement, quotation, an example or illustration, humorous anecdote, a suspenseful observation, or a compliment to the reader. You must do this at the very beginning of your letter – not near the end which may never get read or where the reader's attention span has dissipated. You should always present your most important points first.

2. **Persuade the reader about you, the product:** Good advertising copy involves the reader in the product by stressing **value and benefits**. It tells why the reader should acquire the product. A good job search letter should do the same – the product is you and the letter should stress the specific benefits the reader will receive for contacting you. The benefits you should offer are your skills and accomplishments as they relate to the reader's present and future needs. Therefore, you must know something about your reader's needs before you can offer the proper mix of benefits.

3. **Convince the reader with more evidence:** Good advertising copy presents facts about the product that relate to its benefits. An effective job search letter should also present evidence of the writer's benefits. Statements of specific accomplishments and examples of productivity are the strongest such evidence.

4. **Move the reader to take action (acquire the product):** Effective advertising copy concludes with a call to take action to acquire the product. This usually involves a convenient order form or a toll free telephone number. To stress the benefits of the product without moving the reader to take action would be a waste of time and money. When writing job search letters, you should conclude with a call to action. This is the ultimate power of paper. You want the reader to do something he or she ordinarily would not do – pick up the telephone to contact you, or write you a positive letter that leads to job search information, advice, and referrals as well as job interviews and offers. But we know few letters are so powerful as to move the reader to take initiative in contacting the letter writer. Simply put, the benefits are not as clear in a job search letter as they are in

selling a product through advertising copy. Therefore, your call to action should mention that **you** will contact the reader by telephone at a certain time.

Form, style, content, production, and distribution all play important roles in communicating these persuasive elements in your letters.

TIP #164
Be sure to properly plan and organize your letters.

It goes without saying that you need to plan and organize your writing. By all means do not copy or edit a letter you think may be a good example of an effective job search letter. "Canned" letters tend to be too formal. Worst of all, they look and sound canned and thus they lack credibility.

Your letters should represent **you** – your personality, your credibility, your style, and your purpose. Start by asking yourself these questions **before** organizing and writing your letters:

- What is the **purpose** of this letter?
- What are the **needs** of my audience?
- What is a good opening sentence or paragraph for grabbing the **attention** of my audience?
- How can I maintain the **interest** of my audience?
- How can I best end the letter so that my audience will be **persuaded** to contact me?
- How much **time** should I spend revising and proofreading the letter?
- Will this letter represent my **best professional effort**?

After writing your letter, review these questions again. But this time convert them into a checklist for evaluating the potential effectiveness of your letter:

- Is the **purpose** of this letter clear?
- Does the letter clearly target the **needs** of my audience?
- Does the opening sentence or paragraph grab the **attention** of my audience?

- Does the letter state specific **benefits** for the reader?
- Does the letter sustain the **interest** of my audience?
- Will the letter **persuade** the reader to contact me?
- Have I spent enough **time** revising and proofreading the letter?
- Does the letter represent my **best professional effort?**

Always keep in mind what you want your audience to do in reference to your job search:

- Pay attention to your message.
- Remember you.
- Take specific actions you want taken.

TIP #165
Select a letter style that works best for you.

You basically have four different styles to choose from – semi-blocked, modified-blocked, fully-blocked, or square-blocked. We prefer the fully-blocked style where all paragraphs begin left-flush. However, the other styles also work well. We also prefer left-justifying our letters. Fully justified letters look too formal and mass produced. However, whether you left-justify or fully justify your letters may not make a difference in terms of outcomes – getting invited to interviews. Select a style, be consistent, and concentrate on producing high impact letter **content**.

TIP #166
Avoid lengthy letters.

Try to keep your letters to one page. However, if a letter runs two pages, be sure it doesn't overwhelm your resume. The principle of "less is more" is applicable to both your resume and letter.

TIP #167
Keep your cover letter focused on what's important.

Express your interest in the position, state your most important skills and achievements in direct reference to the employer's skill requirements, and say when you will call the employer. Make sure the tone of your letter is very employer-centered, enthusiastic, and energetic.

TIP #168
The body of your letter should observe
12 key content rules.

The body of the letter should clearly communicate your message. How well you structure this section of the letter will largely determine how much impact it will have on your reader. You want to make sure the content of your letter speaks clearly to the needs of the reader.

The basic principles of effective communication are especially applicable to the body of your letter. In general you should:

1. **Have a clear purpose in writing your letter:** First ask yourself *"What message do I want to convey to my reader? What do I want him or her to do after reading my letter?"* Your message should be directly related to some desirable action or outcome.

2. **Plan and organize each section:** Each paragraph should be related to your overall purpose as well as to each other. The message should be logical and flow in sequential order. Start with a detailed outline of your message.

3. **Put your most important ideas first:** Since readers' attention decreases in direct relation to the length of a message, always state your most important points first.

4. **Keep your paragraphs short and your sentences simple:** Your reader is most likely a busy person who does not have time to read and interpret long and complex letters. The shorter the letter the better. Plain simple English is always preferred to complex usages which require the reader to re-read and decode your language. Three to four paragraphs, each three to five lines in length, should be sufficient. Keep sentences to no more than 25 words. Avoid including too many ideas in a single sentence.

5. **Your opening sentence should get the attention of the reader:** Your first sentence is the most important one. It should have a similar function as an advertisement – get the

interest and involvement of your audience. Avoid the standard canned openers by making your sentence unique.

6. **Your opening paragraph should clearly communicate
   your purpose:** Get directly to the point in as short a space
   as possible. Remember, this is a business letter. Your reader
   wants to know why he should spend time reading your letter.
   Your first sentence should tell why and begin motivating him
   or her to take actions you desire.

7. **Your letter should convince the reader to take action:**
   Most letters function to inform and/or to persuade. In either
   case, they should lead to some action. Incorporate the four
   principles of good advertising in your letter writing:

   - Catch the reader's attention.
   - Persuade the reader about you or your product – establish
     your credibility.
   - Convince the reader with more evidence and benefits.
   - Move the reader to acquire the service or product.

8. **Follow rules of good grammar, spelling, and punctuation:** Grammatical, spelling, and punctuation errors communicate a lack of competence and professionalism. Always
   check and re-check for such errors by (1) proofreading the
   letter yourself at least twice, and (2) asking someone else to
   proofread it also.

9. **Communicate your unique style:** Try to avoid standard or
   "canned" business language which is found in numerous
   how-to books on business writing and sample letters. Such
   language tends to be too formalistic and boring. Some examples go to the other extreme in presenting excessively aggressive and obnoxious letters which would turn off any normal
   employer. Write as if you were talking to a reader in a
   natural conversational tone. Be honest and straightforward
   in your message. Use your imagination in making your letter
   interesting. Put your personality into this letter. Try to
   demonstrate your **energy and enthusiasm** through your

writing tone. For example, what type of impression does this letter leave on a reader?

> I'm writing in response to your recent ad for an assistant manager at your Great Falls Super store.
>
> Please find enclosed a copy of my resume which outlines my experience in relationship to this position.
>
> Thank you for your consideration.

This is a typical cover letter received by many employers. While this letter is short and to the point, it doesn't grab the reader's attention, sustain his interest, nor move him to action. It screams "b-o-r-i-n-g!" It sounds like hundreds of canned cover letters employers receive each day. Why not try writing with more personality and energy? Consider this alternative:

> Last year I increased profits by 15 percent at Star Drugs. It was a tremendous challenge, but the secret was simple – conduct the company's first management review which resulted in reorganizing the pharmaceutical and video sections. We eliminated two full-time employees and dramatically improved customer service.
>
> I'm now interested in taking on a similar challenge with another company interested in improving its productivity. When I saw your ad in Sunday's Toledo Star, I thought we might share a mutual interest.
>
> If you're interested in learning more about my experience, let's talk soon on how we might work together. I'll call you Thursday afternoon to answer any questions. In the meantime, please look over my enclosed resume.

Which letter do you think will grab the attention of the employer and lead to some action? The first letter is both standard and boring. The second letter, equally true, incorporates most principles of effective letter writing – and advertising!

10. **Be personable by referring to "you" more than "I" or "we"**: Your letters should communicate that you are other-

centered rather than self-centered. You communicate your awareness and concern for the individual by frequently referring to "you."

11. **Try to be positive in what you say:** Avoid negative words and tones in your letters. Such words as "can't," "didn't," "shouldn't," and "won't" should be eliminated and replaced with more positive terms for stating a negative. For example, instead of writing:

> I don't have the required five years experience nor have I taken the certification test.

Try putting your message in a more positive tone by using positive content:

> I have several years of experience and will be taking the certification test next month.

12. **Follow the basic ABC's of good writing:** These consist of Always Being:

- Clear
- Correct
- Complete
- Concise
- Courteous
- Considerate
- Creative
- Cheerful
- Careful

TIP #169
Be selective in what you include and exclude in your letters.

What should be included and omitted in your cover letters? This question depends on your purpose and your audience. If you are responding to a vacancy announcement or a classified ad, you need to address the stated requirements for submitting an application. This usually involves a resume and sometimes information on your "salary requirements."

Use the following general guidelines when trying to decide what to include or omit in your letters:

Things you should include:

- Positive information that supports your candidacy.
- Information on your skills, abilities, strengths, accomplishments, interests, and goals.
- Examples of your productivity and performance.
- Benefits you can offer the reader.
- A daytime contact telephone number.

Things you should omit:

- Any extraneous information unrelated to the position, the employer's needs, or your skills.
- Any negative references to a former employer, your weaknesses, or the employer's organization and position.
- Boastful statements or proposed solutions to employer's problems.
- Salary requirements or history.
- References.
- Personal information such as height, weight, marital status, hobbies – information that also should not appear on a resume.

TIP #170
Address your letter to a real person by name.

Always try (make a phone call) to get the name of a specific person to whom you should address your letter, resume, and follow-up phone call. Without a name, you will have difficulty conducting a follow-up. However, if you are unable to get a name, or if your inquiries result in instructions *to "just send it to Personnel or Human Resources, "*send your correspondence to the required department. Avoid standard anonymous salutations such as "Dear Sir/Madam" or "To Whom It May Concern." We prefer leaving the salutation off altogether and go directly from your return address at the top to the body of your letter.

TIP #171
Direct your letter to the appropriate person.

Most personnel and human resources departments do not make hiring decisions. They may announce vacancies, process paperwork, handle benefits, and hire for positions within their departments, but most do not hire for positions in other departments. You need to research the organization and find out who makes the hiring decisions in your occupational area and then address your letter to that individual. The person who usually has the power to hire is found in an operational unit that has the actual hiring need. This also is the person, or persons, who will interview candidates. You will waste your time and effort by sending an unsolicited resume and letter to personnel or human resources.

TIP #172
Use strong openers in your letters.

Open with an attention-grabbing question or statement. For example, *"Are you looking for someone who can increase sales by 30 percent a year? I have done so for the past five years as . . ."* Whatever you do, avoid such standard openers as *"Please find enclosed a copy of my resume in response to . . ."* This is a dull and formal opener that may stop the reader at the end of the first sentence. It does not separate you from the competition. It does little to express your enthusiasm, energy, and personality. It's simply deadly and may kill your resume!

TIP #173
Carefully craft and proofread every word,
sentence, and paragraph.

Like the resume, your letters should be picture perfect – no misspellings or grammatical errors. Be sure to proofread your letters very carefully. Also, have someone else read your letters for errors and content. This is especially important if you are sending letters by e-mail. Avoid quickly composing e-mails and hitting the send button. Always carefully proofread your e-mails – treat them like a well-crafted paper letter.

TIP #174
Avoid repeating the content of your resume
in a cover letter.

Too many job seekers merely repeat the content of their resume in the cover letter. A cover letter should include unique content – things that are not included in the resume. Most important of all, in this letter you have the opportunity to express certain desirable qualities not evident in most resumes – your unique personality, energy, and enthusiasm. The cover letter should be designed to persuade the reader to take action, which means inviting you to the interview.

TIP #175
Avoid using canned language in your letters.

Employers normally receive the same types of uninspired job search letters – job seekers tend to use canned language that appears to be taken from a book on letter writing. Few such letters grab the attention of readers and persuade them to respond positively to the writer. Such cover letter phrases as *"Please find enclosed . . . ," "I'm pleased to learn about . . . ," "As summarized in the enclosed resume . . . ," "I appreciate your consideration," "I look forward to hearing from you,"* and *"Please give me a call if you have any questions"*

> *Your cover letter should be designed to persuade the reader to invite you to the interview.*

are good indications of canned and uninspired language. Again, make sure your letters express your unique personality, energy, and enthusiasm. Be different and bold – write a letter that truly reveals who you are in terms of interests, skills, and goals; orient it toward taking action. Let the employer know you are different from the competition and that you really want the job.

TIP #176
Use positive and performance-oriented language
throughout your letters.

Similar to the choice of language throughout your job search and on your resume (Tips #90 and #94), you want to impress upon the employer that you are a performer who has a pattern of performance – someone who regularly achieves results. In so doing, you need to provide examples, stories, and statistics of your achievements. Avoid any negative language that could be misinterpreted as a potential red flag.

TIP #177
Structure your cover letter for action.

Keep your cover letter short and to the point. Three paragraphs should suffice:

1. State your interest and purpose. Try to link your interests to the employer's needs.

2. Highlight your enclosed resume by stressing what you will do for the employer in reference to the employer's specific needs.

3. Request an interview and indicate that you will call soon to schedule an appointment.

Let the employer know you are different from the competition and that you really want the job.

On the next page we include a good example of such a letter written in response to a specific job vacancy. It is purposeful without being overly aggressive or boastful. The writer's purpose is already known by the employer. The first paragraph should restate the position listed as well as the source of information. It links the writer's interests to the employer's needs. The writer also indicates knowledge of the organization. Overall, the first paragraph is succinct, purposeful, and thoughtful. The writer invites the reader to learn more about him.

In the second paragraph the writer generates additional interest by referring to his enclosed resume and including additional information for emphasizing his qualifications vis-a-vis the employer's needs. The writer also attempts to re-write the employer's ad around his qualifications. In so doing, this writer should stand out from other candidates, because he **raises** the expectations of the employer beyond the position description.

931 Davis Street
Boston, MA 01931
January 18, _____

John F. Baird, Manager
Hopkins International Corporation
7532 Grand Avenue
Boston, MA 01937

Dear Mr. Baird:

Your listing in the January 17 issue of the <u>Daily News</u> for a managerial trainee interests me for several reasons. I possess the necessary experience and skills you outline in the ad. Your company has a fine reputation for quality products and a track record of innovation and growth. I seek a challenging position which will fully use my talents.

My experience and skills are summarized in the enclosed resume. You may be interested in several additional qualifications. I would bring to this position:

- the ability to relate well to others
- a record of accomplishments and a desire to achieve better results
- a willingness to take on new responsibilities
- enthusiasm and initiative

I would appreciate more information concerning this position as well as an opportunity to meet with you to discuss our mutual interests. I will call you Thursday morning concerning any questions we both may have and to arrange an interview if we deem it is appropriate at that time.

I appreciate your consideration and look forward to meeting you.

Sincerely yours,

Steven Reeves

Steven Reeves

The writer, in effect, suggests to the employer that they will be getting more for their money than anticipated. This paragraph does not appear hyped, boastful, or aggressive. It is low-keyed yet assertive.

In the third paragraph of this example, the writer makes an open-ended offer to the employer which is difficult to refuse. Linking his interest to the reader's, the writer softens the interview request without putting the employer on the spot of having to say "yes" or "no." Overall, the writer presents the employer with an opportunity to examine his **value**. Accompanied by an outstanding resume, this letter should make a positive impression on the employer. A phone call within 48 hours of receiving the letter will further enhance the writer's candidacy.

TIP #178
Make your letters unique by expressing your personality, energy, and enthusiasm.

Resumes follow a standard screening format that emphasizes descriptive information organized into standard resume categories. The main focus of resumes is on providing details on a candidate's goals, education, and work history. Except for the crisp and succinct language for detailing such information, resumes say little about the personality and behavior of individuals. On the other hand, job search letters provide candidates with opportunities to express their unique personality, energy, and enthusiasm – key values and qualities sought by many employers. Be sure to craft a unique letter that expresses such qualities to prospective employers.

TIP #179
Print your letter on the same paper as your resume.

Everything should match, including the envelope. Remember, you're demonstrating your best professional effort in your paper presentation. Matching papers present a good professional image. However, should you choose a special resume paper, such as a light gray paper with a white border, print your accompanying cover letter on matching white paper.

TIP #180
Avoid putting salary information in your letter.

If an employment ad asks you to state your "salary history," then include it in your letter. But calculate your total compensation package which could be 45% above your yearly salary figure. In the case of "salary requirements," state "open" or "negotiable." You want to negotiate your salary requirements based upon (1) demonstrating your value to the employer during the interview and (2) learning the value of the position in question. And when you do get to the negotiation stage, make sure your "salary requirements" are stated as a range rather than a specific dollar figure. By stating a range, you leave room to negotiate a higher salary than an employer may initially offer.

TIP #181
Be careful what you include with your letter other than a resume.

Include nothing with your resume and letter unless requested by the employer. Sending unsolicited photos, transcripts, and samples of work distracts from your message and makes you look desperate. Such items would be more appropriate to include in a "portfolio." Include them only if requested to do so.

TIP #182
Print your letter on the same size paper as your resume.

A smaller size paper tends to communicate a more personal message. Remember, this is business correspondence that should demonstrate your best professional effort.

TIP #183
Send your correspondence by regular mail.

Unless you are requested to send your letter by e-mail, send it by regular mail. In some occupations, such as sales, an unusual letter in the form of a telegram may get you special attention and thus would be perfectly acceptable. However, in other occupational areas, especially more conservative circles, writing a conventional letter and sending it by conventional means is more appropriate. If you want to get special attention, mail your letter using a Federal Express, UPS, Express Mail, or other special delivery envelope. However, in many cases your correspondence will first go to a mail room where it may be opened and then routinely forwarded to the appropriate person who never sees your special delivery efforts! Consequently, it's uncertain if the extra costs of such a mailing is worth it.

TIP #184
Include a follow-up/action statement indicating what you intend to do next.

A letter without an action statement is a relatively ineffective job search letter. Without being overly aggressive, you can suggest an appropriate time for discussing your candidacy. This is usually done in the closing paragraph of an approach or cover letter. An effective statement goes something like this:

> *"I'll give you a call the afternoon of October 7th to answer any questions you might have concerning my candidacy."*

Without such an action statement, you may not hear from the employer. By closing with an action statement, you indicate that you are a "heads-up" candidate who needs to be **read and remembered** because you will be calling soon. If and when you include such follow-up statements, be sure you actually follow up. If not, such a statement becomes ineffective.

TIP #185
Conduct both internal and external evaluations that incorporate key organization, design, writing, production, distribution, and follow-up principles.

Be sure to conduct two types of evaluations related to your letters. The first is an **internal evaluation**. This is a self-evaluation you conduct by examining your actions in reference to specific performance criteria.

The second type of evaluation may be more important than the internal evaluation. This is an **external evaluation** which is conducted by someone other than yourself. You ask individuals whose judgment you respect to give you feedback on your job search actions. In the case of letters, you want to find two or three individuals who will read your letters and then give you frank feedback on your writing strengths and weaknesses. This external evaluation is the closest you will get to receiving realistic feedback from the actual letter recipient.

Internal Evaluation

Once you complete your first job search letter, conduct a thorough internal evaluation based upon the following criteria. Several of these criteria relate to each step in the letter writing process – structure, organization, production, distribution, and follow-up activities. Respond to each statement by circling the appropriate number to the right that most accurately describes your letter.

Audience	Yes	Maybe	No
1. I know the needs of my audience based upon my research of both the organization and the individual.	1	2	3
2. My letter clearly reflects an understanding of the needs of the organization and the letter recipient.	1	2	3
3. The letter recipient will remember me favorably based on the unique style and content of my letter.	1	2	3
4. My letter speaks the language of the employer – goals and benefits.	1	2	3

Form, Structure, and Design

	Yes	Maybe	No
5. Makes an immediate good impression and is inviting to read.	1	2	3
6. First seven elements in letter (heading, date line, inside address, salutation, body, closing, signature lines) are present and adhere to the rules.	1	2	3
7. Body subdivided into 2-4 paragraphs.	1	2	3
8. Most paragraphs run no more than 5 lines.	1	2	3
9. Most sentences are 25 words or fewer in length.	1	2	3

10. Includes complete name and address of
    letter recipient.   1   2   3

11. Signed name looks strong and confident
    using a fountain or liquid ink pen.   1   2   3

12. Selected a standard type style.   1   2   3

13. Has a clean, crisp, uncluttered, and
    professional look.   1   2   3

14. Used a 1¼" to 1½" margin around the
    top, bottom and sides.   1   2   3

15. Confined to a single page.   1   2   3

Organization and Content

16. Immediately grabs the reader's attention.   1   2   3

17. Presents most important ideas first.   1   2   3

18. Expressed concisely.   1   2   3

19. Relates to the reader's interests and needs.   1   2   3

20. Persuades the reader to take action.   1   2   3

21. Free of spelling, grammatical, and
    punctuation errors.   1   2   3

22. Incorporates the active voice.   1   2   3

23. Avoids negative words and tones; uses
    positive language throughout.   1   2   3

24. Expresses the "unique you."   1   2   3

25. Employer-centered rather than self-centered.   1   2   3

26. Stresses benefits the reader is likely to
    receive from the letter writer.   1   2   3

27. Demonstrates a clear purpose.   1   2   3

28. Sentences and paragraphs flow logically.   1   2   3

29. Includes complete contact information
    (no P.O. Box numbers).   1   2   3

30. Expresses enthusiasm, energy, and fire.   1   2   3

31. Follows the ABC's of good writing.   1   2   3

Production Quality

32. Has an overall strong professional
    appearance sufficient to make an
    immediate favorable impression.   1   2   3

33. Used a new or nearly new ribbon (if
    cloth) with clean keys or printer head.   1   2   3

34. Adjusted copy setting properly – not
    too dark, not too light.   1   2   3

35. Type appears neat, clean, and straight.   1   2   3

36. Printed with a standard type style and size.   1   2   3

37. Produced on a letter quality machine.   1   2   3

38. Proofread and ran "spell-check" (if
    using a word processing program) for
    possible spelling/typing errors.   1   2   3

39. Used good quality paper stock that both
    looks and feels professional.   1   2   3

40. Selected a paper color appropriate for
    my audience.   1   2   3

41. Compared to nine other business letters
    received over the past year, this is one of
    three best in appearance.   1   2   3

Distribution

42. Addressed to a specific name.   1   2   3

43. Used a No. 10 business or a 9 x 12
    inch envelope.   1   2   3

44. Checked to make sure all enclosures
    got enclosed.   1   2   3

45. Matched the envelope paper stock and
    color to the stationery.   1   2   3

46. Typed the address and return address.   1   2   3

47. Affixed a commemorative stamp.   1   2   3

48. Used a special delivery service for
    overnight delivery.   1   2   3

49. Followed-up letter immediately with
    a phone call.   1   2   3

Follow-Up Actions

50. Completed the "Job Search Contract."
    (on page 17)   1   2   3

51. Completed my first "Weekly Job Search
    Performance and Planning Report."
    (on page 18)   1   2   3

52. Ended my letter with an action statement
    indicating I would contact the individual
    by phone within the next week.   1   2   3

53. Made the first follow-up call at the
    time and date indicated in my letter.   1   2   3

54. Followed-up with additional phone calls until
    I was able to speak directly with the person
    or received the requested information.   1   2   3

55. Maintained a positive and professional
    attitude during each follow-up activity. Was
    pleasantly persistent and tactful during all
    follow-up calls. Never indicated I was
    irritated, insulted, or disappointed in not
    having my phone calls returned.   1   2   3

56. Followed-up the follow-up by sending a thank you letter genuinely expressing my appreciation for the person's time and information.   1   2   3

TOTAL
```
┌──────────────┐
│              │
└──────────────┘
```

Add the numbers you circled to the right of each statement to get a cumulative score. If your score is higher than 60, you need to work on improving your letter effectiveness. Go back and institute the necessary changes to create a dynamite letter.

External Evaluation

You can best conduct an external evaluation of your letters by circulating them to two or more individuals. Choose people whose opinions are objective, frank, and thoughtful. Do not select friends and relatives who usually flatter you with positive comments. Professional acquaintances or people you don't know personally but whom you admire may be good evaluators. An ideal evaluator has experience in hiring people in your area of job interest. In addition to sharing their experience with you, they may refer you to other individuals who would be interested in your qualifications. If you choose such individuals to critique both your letter and resume (see Tip #107 for resume evaluations), ask them for their frank reaction – not what they would politely say to a candidate sending these materials. You want them to role play with you, an interview candidate. Ask your evaluators:

- How would you react to this letter if you received it from a candidate? Does it grab your attention and interest you enough to talk with me?

- If you were writing this letter, what changes would you make? Any additions, deletions, or modifications?

You should receive good cooperation and advice by approaching people for this external evaluation. In addition, you will probably get valuable unsolicited advice on other job search matters, such as job leads, job market information, and employment strategies.

In contrast to the closed and deductive nature of the internal evaluation, the external evaluation should be open-ended and inductive. Let your reader give you as much information as possible on the quality and potential impact of your letter. Taken together, the internal and external evaluations should complement each other and provide you with maximum information.

Appendix A

Resume Worksheets

THE FOLLOWING PAGES include basic worksheets for generating the necessary data for constructing each section of your resume and preparing important job search documents:

- Employment Experience
- Military Experience
- Community/Civic/Volunteer Experience
- Educational Data
- Additional Information

Complete each of these forms as thoroughly as possible. You will probably need to make extra copies of the "Employment Experience Worksheet" on page 182 since you will need to complete one form for each job you held.

Completing these forms will result in a large amount of useful information about yourself. While you will not use all the information you include on these worksheets, such as earnings, you will have a relatively comprehensive database from which to write the most important sections of your resume, complete applications, craft targeted letters, and prepare for the critical job interview.

Employment Experience Worksheet

1. Name of employer:_____

2. Address: _____

   _____

3. Inclusive dates of employment: from _____ to _____.
                                        month/year   month/year

4. Type of organization: _____

5. Size of organization/approximate number of employees: _____

6. Approximate annual sales volume or annual budget: _____

7. Position held: _____

8. Earnings per month/year: _____

9. Responsibilities/duties: _____

   _____

   _____

   _____

10. Achievements or significant contributions: _____

    _____

    _____

11. Demonstrated skills and abilities: _____

    _____

    _____

12. Reason(s) for leaving: _____

    _____

Military Experience Worksheet

1. Service: _____

2. Rank: _____

3. Inclusive dates: from _____ to _____ .

                                 month/year   month/year

4. Responsibilities/duties: _____

   _____

   _____

   _____

   _____

5. Significant contributions/achievements: _____

   _____

   _____

   _____

   _____

   _____

6. Demonstrated skills and abilities: _____

   _____

   _____

   _____

   _____

   _____

7. Reserve status: _____

Community/Civic/Volunteer Experience

1. Name and address of organization/group: _____

    _____

    _____

    _____

2. Inclusive dates: from _____ to _____.
                              month/year   month/year

3. Offices held/nature of involvement: _____

    _____

    _____

    _____

4. Significant contributions/achievements/projects: _____

    _____

    _____

    _____

    _____

    _____

5. Demonstrated skills and abilities: _____

    _____

    _____

    _____

    _____

    _____

Educational Data

1. Institution: _____

2. Address: _____

_____

3. Inclusive dates: from _____ to _____.
   　　　　　　　　　　　month/year　　　　　　　month/year

4. Degree or years completed: _____

5. Major: _____ Minor(s): _____

6. Education highlights: _____

_____

_____

7. Student activities: _____

_____

_____

8. Demonstrated abilities and skills: _____

_____

_____

9. Significant contributions/achievements: _____

_____

_____

_____

10. Special training courses: _____

_____

11. G.P.A.: _____ (on _____ index)
    　　　　　　　　　　point

Additional Information

1. Professional memberships and status:

 a. _____

 b. _____

 c. _____

 d. _____

2. Licenses/certifications:

 a. _____

 b. _____

 c. _____

3. Expected salary range: $ _____ to $ _____ (but do not include this on your resume)

4. Acceptable amount of on-the-job travel: _____ days per month.

5. Areas of acceptable relocation:

 a. _____ c. _____

 b. _____ d. _____

6. Date of availability: _____

7. Contacting present employer:

 a. Is he or she aware of your prospective job change? _____

 b. May he or she be contacted at this time? _____

8. References: (name, address, telephone number, e-mail address – not on resume)

 a. _____ c. _____

 b. _____ d. _____

9. Foreign languages and degree of competency:

     a. _____

     b. _____

10. Interests and activities: hobbies, avocations, pursuits

     a. _____

     b. _____

     c. _____

     d. _____

     Circle letter of ones which support your objective.

11. Foreign travel:

	Country	Purpose	Dates
a.	_____	_____	_____
b.	_____	_____	_____
c.	_____	_____	_____

12. Special awards/recognition:

     a. _____

     b. _____

     c. _____

13. Special abilities/skills/talents/accomplishments:

     a. _____

     b. _____

     c. _____

Appendix B

Resume Examples

THE FOLLOWING RESUME examples incorporate numerous resume writing tips outlined in Chapters 3 and 4. We've selected some of the best resume examples which are showcased in three of our other resume and letter books: *Military Resumes and Cover Letters*, *Nail the Resume!*, and *High Impact Resumes and Letters* (Impact Publications). Some of these resumes were developed by professional resume writers who can be found by following the advice outlined in Tip #21 and #51. Our contributors include:

Louise Garver (pages 202-203)
www.CareerDirectionsLLC.com

Susan Guarneri (pages 204-205)
www.resume-magic.com

Janice M. Shepherd (pages 206-207)
www.writeoncareerkeys.com

Use these examples to get ideas for writing your own resume. Avoid creatively plagiarizing such examples. Your resume should always represent the "unique you."

JOHN ALBERT
1099 Seventh Avenue
Akron, OH 44522
322-645-8271

OBJECTIVE: A position as **architectural drafter** with a firm specializing in commercial construction where technical knowledge and practical experience will enhance construction design and building operations.

EXPERIENCE: <u>Draftsman</u>: Akron Construction Company, Akron, OH. Helped develop construction plans for $24 million of residential and commercial construction. (2003 to present)

<u>Cabinet Maker</u>: Jason's Linoleum & Carpet Company, Akron, OH. Designed and constructed kitchen counter tops and cabinets; installed the material in homes; cut and laid linoleum flooring in apartment complexes. (1997 to 2002)

<u>Carpenter's Assistant</u>: Kennison Associates, Akron, OH. Assisted carpenter in the reconstruction of a restaurant and in building of forms for pouring concrete. (Summer 1996)

<u>Materials Control Auditor</u>: Taylor Machine and Foundry, Akron, OH. Collected data on the amount of material being utilized daily in the operation of the foundry. Evaluated the information to determine the amount of materials being wasted. Submitted reports to production supervisor on the analysis of weekly and monthly production. (Summer 1995)

TRAINING: <u>Drafting School, Akron Vocational and Technical Center</u>, 1999. Completed 15 months of training in drafting night school.

EDUCATION: <u>Akron Community High School</u>, Akron, OH. Graduated in 1998.

PERSONAL: Single...willing to relocate...prefer working both indoors and outdoors...strive for perfection...hard worker...enjoy photography, landscaping, furniture design and construction.

REFERENCES: Available upon request.

David Watson
2211 Bailey Drive
Houston, Texas 77777
Tel. 123-456-9876
E-mail: davidw@wireme.com

Objective

A challenging position using skills in **Financial Analysis, Security Analysis, Budget Analysis,** and **Investment Strategies** that will be used to:

- strengthen a company's financial position
- identify new investment opportunities
- develop effective financial strategies
- manage future performance

Qualifications Summary

Detail- and results-oriented individual with strong analytical and entrepreneurial skills in accounting and financial systems. Adept at using statistical and other forecasting models for creating budgets, improving business operations, and developing investment strategies. Proven ability to create and implement effective cost management systems. Over 8 years of progressive responsibility and expertise in financial environments dealing with:

Financial Analysis/Planning	Investment Analysis	Accounting
Strategic Planning	Cash Management	Contracting
Credit Analysis	Budget Analysis	Valuation
Mergers and Acquisitions	Financial Management	Research
E-commerce	Risk Management	Project Management

Experience and Accomplishments

Finance

- Managed financial operation of government contractor with $15 million in assets and $25 million in annual revenue. **Results:** Saved over $50,000 in annual accounting costs by strengthening leadership over all accounting, payroll, banking, and risk management functions.

- Analyzed financial statements and other related reports, using ratio analysis to identify possible weaknesses in the company's financial operations and recommended remedial actions. **Results:** Improved procedures enabled company to develop aggressive marketing strategy for generating an additional $5 million in revenue.

- Developed and administered new defined contribution, profit sharing, and cafeteria plans. **Results:** Employee turnover reduced by 20 percent over a 12-month period.

- Prepared reports that summarized and forecasted company business activity based on past, present, and expected operations. Used various forecasting techniques, such as regression, moving averages, and other econometric models, to establish the forecasted figures. **Results:** Earnings forecasts, which were 95 percent accurate in the first six months, established new investment strategy for a 20 percent annual growth rate.

- Created the operational, cash, and capital budgets of several small companies. Introduced simplified small business accounting software programs to manage day-to-day accounting functions. **Results:** Saved each business over $30,000 annually by eliminating the need to hire a full-time accountant.

David Watson   Page 2

Accounting

- Defended employer before Contract Board of Appeals. **Results:** Saved employer over $200,000 in disallowed contract costs emanating from a FTAC audit.

- Performed all facets of accounting, including accounts payable, receivable, payroll functions, and general ledger account reconciliation and bank reconciliation statements. **Results:** Eliminated the need for two part-time bookkeeping positions and thus saved employer over $40,000 a year in personnel costs.

- Prepared corporate financial statements, including income statements, balance sheets, and cash flow statements for both internal and external reporting. **Results:** Improved on-time reporting by 300% within first six months and developed attractive financial portfolio for generating $8 million in outside investment.

- Introduced a budgetary system that inculcated a culture of cost control awareness. **Results:** Streamlined the service delivery system of a training company and saved over $100,000 annually in wasteful processes.

- Developed sensitivity models for determining break-even sales volume for each corporate division. **Results:** Improved profitability of five divisions by 15 percent within six months and eliminated one unprofitable division which saved the company more than $200,000.

Professional Experience

DELTA COMPUTER SERVICES, Orlando, FL	2003 – Present
Controller	
THE TRAINING GROUP, Atlanta, GA	1998 – 2002
Senior Accountant	
SEVEN SMALL BUSINESSES	1992 – Present
Part-time consultant in various aspects of accounting	

Education

University of Illinois	MBA, Finance	1999

- Developed award-winning e-commerce business model for reaching undergraduate students
- Interned with KPMG as Investment Analyst

Vanderbilt University	BA, Accounting	1994

- Graduated with Honors, 3.8/4.0
- Worked full-time in earning 100% of educational and personal expenses

Computer Skills

- Microsoft Word
- Excel
- Access
- PowerPoint
- PageMaker
- PhotoShop
- Lotus Notes

Memberships and Affiliations

- Society of Investment Analysts
- American Society of Accountants
- American Association of Individual Investors
- Toastmasters International

MARY FURNISS
7812 W. 24th Street   821-879-1124
Dallas, TX 71234   furnissm@aol.com

OBJECTIVE: **A management position** involving the application of computer
technology for improving the efficiency of publishing operations.

EXPERIENCE: <u>Computer Applications Manager, 2003 to present</u>
Stevens Publishing Company, Fort Worth, TX

Managed all computer-related projects for publishing firm with
annual sales of $40 million. Presented yearly capital expenditure
and general systems budget, negotiated computer service contracts,
evaluated and recommended new equipment and software pur-
chases, and trained staff to use software and hardware. Replaced
ATEX typesetting with desktop publishing system that immediately saved the company $650,000 in operational costs.

<u>Editorial/Production Supervisor, 2000-2002</u>
Benton Publishing Company, San Francisco, CA

Supervised all computer-related projects. Trained staff of 27 to use
WordPerfect and other software applications. Devised an innovative system that transformed traditional galley editing into an
efficient electronic editing system. New computerized system
eliminated the need for two additional employees to handle the
traditional galley editing system. Reduced errors by 70 percent.

<u>Editorial Assistant, 1998-1999</u>
Benton Publishing Company, San Francisco, CA

Prepared annual *Encyclopedia of International Forestry* materials
for editing and production. Supervised freelancers for special
editorial projects. Proofread and copy-edited materials for 18
books produced annually. Received "Employee of the Year" award
for initiating a new computerized editing system that saved the
company $70,000 in annual freelance editing fees.

EDUCATION: <u>University of Washington</u>
B.A., Journalism, 1998.

SPECIAL   Familiar with the ATEX typesetting system and the application
SKILLS: of Ventura desktop publishing software. Attended two advanced
training programs in the use of computerized editing systems.

PERSONAL: Enjoy developing innovative and cost-saving approaches to traditional publishing tasks that involve the application of computer
technology. Work well in team settings and with training groups.
Willing to relocate for the appropriate challenge.

JAMES BARSTOW

7781 West Gate Road
Cincinnati, OH 44411

421-827-0841
barstowj@aol.com

OBJECTIVE

A challenging project manager position involving all phases of construction where a demonstrated record of timely and cost-effective completion of projects is important to both the company and its clients.

SUMMARY OF QUALIFICATIONS

- 28 years of progressively responsible construction management experience involving all facets of construction, from start-up to final inspection.
- Experienced in supervising all aspects of construction including masonry, concrete work, carpentry, electrical, mechanical, and plumbing.
- Communicate and work well with individuals at all levels from client to architect to subcontractors.

EXPERIENCE

Independent Contractor, Barstow & Thomas, Cincinnati, OH

Owned and managed a general contracting company doing $8 million in commercial construction each year. Performed all estimating, established contacts with subcontractors, purchased specialty items and materials, and handled shop drawings. Managed all time scheduling, monthly and submonthly draws, and guaranties. Hired all superintendents. Completed most jobs within 30 days of projected completion dates and managed to keep costs 5 percent under estimates. 2002 to present.

Job Superintendent, J.P. Snow, Columbus, OH

Supervised all work from start-up to final inspection as well as established all time schedules from start to finish. Handled shop drawings, lab testing, job testing, change orders, daily reports, job progress reports, payroll, and hiring. Worked with client, architect, and city, state, and federal inspectors. Responsible for all concrete and carpentry work including piers, beams, slabs, paving, walls, curbs, and walkways. Initiated an innovative scheduling system that saved the employer more than $60,000 in projected down-time. Consistently praised for taking initiative, providing exceptional leadership, and communicating well with clients, architects, and subcontactors. 1997-2001.

Subcontractor, Smith & Company, Columbus, OH

Conducted all bidding, estimating, and purchasing for more than 50 commercial masonry projects. Worked with both union and open shop help. Managed payroll for 75 employees during different project phases. Projects included hospitals, churches, schools, office buildings, and retail shops. 1991-1996.

JANET SOUTHERN

721 James Court
Chicago, IL 60029

401-281-9472
southernj@aol.com

OBJECTIVE: **An accounting/finance position** where analytic and computer skills will be used for managing major accounts and acquiring new corporate clientele.

EXPERIENCE: <u>**Accountant, J.S. Conners & Co., Chicago, IL**</u>
Analyzed accounting systems and installed new IBM ledger system for over 30 corporate accounts. Conducted training programs attended by more than 500 accountants with small businesses. Developed proposals, presented demonstration programs, and prepared reports for corporate clients. Increased new accounts by 42% over a four year period. 2003 to present.

<u>**Junior Accountant, Simon Electrical Co., Chicago, IL**</u>
Acquired extensive experience in all aspects of corporate accounting while assigned to the Controller's Office. Prepared detailed financial records for corporate meetings as well as performed basic accounting tasks such as journal entries, reconciling discrepancies, and checking records for accuracy and consistency. Assisted office in converting to a new computerized accounting system that eliminated the need for additional personnel and significantly improved the accuracy and responsiveness. 1999 to 2002.

<u>**Accounting Clerk, Johnson Supplies, Chicago, IL**</u>
Acquired working knowledge of basic accounting functions for a 200+ employee organization with annual revenues of $45 million. Prepared journal vouchers, posted entries, and completed standard reports. Proposed a backup accounting system that was implemented by the Senior Accountant. 1996 to 1998.

EDUCATION: <u>**Roosevelt University, Chicago, IL**</u>
B.S., Accounting, 1993.
Highlights:
   Minor in Computer Science. Worked as a summer intern with Ballston Accounting Company. Honors graduate with a 3.7/4.0 GPA in all course work.

REFERENCES: Available upon request.

CHARLES DAVIS

771 Anderson Street   421-789-5677
Knoxville, TN 37921   davisc@aol.com

OBJECTIVE: A **paralegal position** with a firm specializing in crimi-
                   nal law where research and writing skills and an atten-
                   tion to detail will be used for completing timely assign-
                   ments.

EDUCATION: **University of Illinois, Champaign, IL**
                   B.A., Criminal Justice, 2005.
                   Highlights:
                     Minor, English
                     President, Paralegal Student Association, 2004.
                     3.7/4.0 GPA

                   Rock Island Junior College, Rock Island, IL
                   A.A., English, 1995.

AREAS OF EFFECTIVENESS

LAW: Completed 36 semester hours of criminal justice course
                   work with special emphasis on criminal law. Served as
                   an intern with law firm specializing in criminal law.
                   Interviewed clients, drafted documents, conducted legal
                   research, assisted lawyers in preparing court briefs.
                   Participated in criminal justice forums sponsored by the
                   Department of Criminal Justice at the University of
                   Illinois.

RESEARCH: Conducted research on several criminal cases as both a
                   student and a paralegal intern. Experienced in examin-
                   ing court cases, interviewing lawyers and judges, and
                   observing court proceedings. Proficient in using micro-
                   fiche and computerized data bases for conducting legal
                   research.

COMMUNICATION: Prepared research papers, legal summaries, and memos
                   and briefed attorneys on criminal cases relevant to as-
                   signments. Used telephone extensively for interviewing
                   clients and conducting legal research.

WORK   **Paralegal Intern, Stanford and Rollins, Peoria, IL.**
EXPERIENCE: Summer Intern, 1996. Assigned to numerous research
                   projects relevant to pending criminal cases.

                   Part-time employment.
                   Held several part-time positions while attending school
                   full-time. These included student assistant in the
                   Department of Criminal Justice, University of Illinois.

JANE BARROWS
997 Mountain Road
Denver, CO 80222

717-349-0137
barrowsj@aol.com

OBJECTIVE:

A manager or assistant manager position with an Accounting Department requiring strong supervisory and communication skills.

EXPERIENCE:

Manager, Accounts Payable, T.L. Dutton, Denver, CO.
Supervised 18 employees who routinely processed 200 invoices a day. Handled vendor inquiries and adjustments. Conducted quarterly accruals and reconciliations. Screened candidates and conducted annual performance evaluations. Reduced the number of billing errors by 30 percent and vendor inquiries by 25% within the first year. 2003 to present.

Supervisor, Accounts Payable, AAA Pest Control, Denver, CO.
Supervised 10 employees who processed nearly 140 invoices a day. Audited vendor invoices, authorized payments, and balanced daily disbursements. Introduced automated accounts receivable system for improving the efficiency and accuracy of receivables. 2000 to 2002.

Bookkeeper, Davis Nursery, Ft. Collins, CO.
Processed accounts payable and receivable, reconciled accounts, balanced daily disbursements, and managed payroll for a 20-employee organization with annual revenues of $1.8 million. 1996 to 1999.

Bookkeeper, Jamison's Lumber, Ft Collins, CO.
Assisted accountant in processing accounts payable and receivable and managing payroll for 40-employee organization with annual revenues of $3.2 million. 1992 to 1995.

EDUCATION:

Colorado Junior College, Denver, CO.
Currently taking advanced courses in accounting, computer science, and management.

Terrance Vo-Tech School, Terrance, CO.
Completed commercial courses, 1991.

REFERENCES:

Available upon request.

SUSAN ALLEN

325 West End Street   402-378-9771
Atlanta, GA 30019   allens@aol.com

OBJECTIVE: **A financial analyst position** with a bank where
experience with investment portfolios will be used
for attracting new clientele.

EXPERIENCE: **Investment Analyst, First City Bank, Atlanta, GA.**
Managed $650 million in diverse portfolios for bank's major
clients which averaged 12 percent annual return on investment. Regularly met with clients, reviewed current invest-
ments, and presented new investment options for further
diversifying portfolios. Introduced biweekly newsletter for
communicating investment strategies with clients and bank
officers. 2003 to present.

Research Analyst, Georgia Bank, Atlanta, GA.
Conducted research, wrote reports, and briefed supervisor on
stock market trends and individual companies which affected
the bank's $1.2 billion securities portfolio. Worked closely
with Investment Analyst in developing new approaches to
communicating research findings and summary reports to
clients and bank officers. 1999 to 2002.

**Research Assistant/Intern, Columbia Savings Bank,
Columbia, SC.**
Served as a Summer Intern while completing undergraduate
degree. Assigned as Research Assistant to Chief Analyst.
Followed stock market trends and conducted research on
selected investment banks. 1996 to 1997.

EDUCATION: **University of Miami, Miami, FL.**
MBA, Business Administration, 1998.
Focused course work on finance and management.
Thesis: "Successful Investment Strategies of Florida's
            Ten Major Banks."

University of South Carolina, Columbia, SC.
B.S., Finance, Department of Commerce, 1996.
Summer Intern with Columbia Savings Bank.
Secretary/Treasurer of the Student Business Association.

REFERENCES: Available upon request.

MARK ABLE

7723 Stevens Avenue   802-461-0921
Phoenix, AZ 80023   ablem@aol.com

OBJECTIVE: **A retail management position** where demonstrated skills
in sales and marketing and enthusiasm for innovation will
be used for improving customer service and expanding department profitability.

SUMMARY OF   Twelve years of progressively responsible experience in
QUALIFICATIONS: all phases of retail sales and marketing with major discount
stores in culturally diverse metropolitan areas. Annually
improved profitability by 15 percent and consistently rated
in top 10 percent of workforce.

EXPERIENCE: **Sales Manager, K-Mart, Memphis, TN**
Managed four departments with annual sales of nearly $8
million. Hired, trained, and supervised a culturally diverse
workforce of 14 full-time and 6 part-time employees.
Reorganized displays, developed new marketing approaches, coordinated customer feedback with buyers in upgrad-
ing quality of merchandise, and improved customer service
that resulted in 25 percent increase in annual sales.
Received "Outstanding" performance evaluation and "Employee of the Year" award. 2003 to present.

Assistant Buyer, Wal-Mart, Memphis, TN
Maintained inventory levels for three departments with
annual sales of $5 million. Developed more competitive
system of vendor relations that reduced product costs by 5
percent. Incorporated latest product and merchandising
trends into purchasing decisions. Worked closely with
department managers in maintaining adequate inventory
levels for best-selling items. 1999 to 2002.

Salesperson, Zayres, Knoxville, TN
Responsible for improving sales in four departments with
annual sales of $3.5 million. Reorganized displays and
instituted new "Ask An Expert" system for improved customer relations. Sales initiatives resulted in a 20 percent
increase in annual sales. Cited for "Excellent customer
relations" in annual performance evaluation. Worked part-
time while completing education. 1996-1998.

EDUCATION: **University of Tennessee, Knoxville, TN**
B.S., Marketing, 1996.
Earned 80 percent of educational expenses while working
part-time and maintaining full course loads.

STEVEN MARSH

2001 West James Court
Seattle, WA 98322

Home: 501-789-4321
Work: 501-789-5539
smarsh@aol.com

OBJECTIVE

A position in aviation law where proven management, organization, and supervisory skills and an exceptional record of success in investigating, adjudicating, settling, defending, and prosecuting cases will be used in settling cases to the benefit of employer and clients.

EXPERIENCE

Chief Circuit Defense Counsel, Davis AFB, Ogden, UT, 2004-Present
Personally defended all Flying Evaluation Boards, winning every one. Successfully defended felony trials covering offenses of drug use, distribution, assault, DUI, and perjury. Supervised, trained, and directed 22 attorneys and 17 paralegals responsible for total defense services across 16 Air Force installations located in 12 states. Included oversight of over 500 trials with every offense up to and including premeditated murder.

Chief, Aviation Settlement Branch, U.S. Air Force, Washington, DC, 2002-2003
Directed the investigation, adjudication, and either settlement or litigation of all aviation, environmental, medical malpractice, and other tort claims filed against the Air Force. In 1993, this topped a $40 billion dollar exposure with the percentage of payout to claimed amount the lowest in over a decade. Supervised staff of 13 attorneys and 5 paralegals. Re-formulated U.S. Air Force policy on tort claim and litigation matters in conjunction with the Department of Justice, leading to a better concept and application of paying the losers and spending time and resources to win the winners.

Chief, Tort Section, U.S. Air Force, Washington, DC, 1999-2001
Supervised the investigation and recommended adjudication or litigation of all aviation tort claims against the Air Force, including the last of the Agent Orange cases and the KAL 007 Korean airliner shoot-down by the Soviet Union. Supervised staff of 3 attorneys and 1 paralegal. Recommended U.S. Air Force policy change on aviation tort claims that directly resulted in greater Agency latitude for meritorious claims independent of the previously required GAO Office requirements.

Staff Judge Advocate, Stevens Air Force Base, Miami, FL, 1997-1998
Advised top management of all legal issues to include the convening of Aircraft Accident Boards and Flying Evaluation Boards. Directed tort, labor, environmental, procurement, and criminal law procedures. During this period, defended two state environmental Notice of Violations successfully, and over 40 criminal cases were prosecuted without a single acquittal. Served as management's Chief Labor Resolution Negotiator securing settlements at 60 percent of the previously approved maximums. Supervised staff of 4 attorneys and 5 paralegals.

Assistant Staff Judge Advocate, Lowry Air Force Base, CO, 1993-1996
Served as government prosecutor for over 35 trials with no acquittals. Served as government representative in over 20 administrative hearings with no losses. Counseled clients on rights/duties under state and federal law.

Area Defense Counsel, Marshall Air Force Base, Austin, TX, 1989-1992
Defended over 300 clients in criminal trials, administrative hearings, or minor disciplinary concerns.

EDUCATION

J.D., Boston University College of Law, Boston, MA, 1983
B.A. (Political Science), University of North Carolina, Chapel Hill, NC, 1980

TRAINING

Air War College, USAF, Seminar Program, 2001
Armed Forces Staff College, Joint Service Program, Residence, 1998
Air Command and Staff College, USAF, Seminar Program, 1997

AWARDS

Stuart Reichart Award, Senior Attorney, HQ USAF, 2000
Ramirez Award, Outstanding Attorney Tactical Air Command, 1996
Outstanding Attorney, U.S. Air Forces Colorado, 1993

OTHER EXPERIENCE

U.S. Parole Board Hearing Member, USAF, 1998
Joint Services Consolidation Committee, 1996-1997

BAR MEMBERSHIPS

U.S. Supreme Court, 2000
U.S. Court of Appeals, 4th Circuit, 1996
U.S. Court of Military Appeals, 1993
Supreme Court of Texas, 1989

MICHAEL RAMIREZ

313 Bradley Drive
Bremerton, WA 90972
W: (206) 222-3333 / H: (206) 888-3321
RamirezM@aol.com

OBJECTIVE

A foreman position where skills and experience as a construction supervisor will benefit a firm seeking to its scope of operations.

QUALIFICATIONS SUMMARY

MANAGEMENT

- Supervised construction crew of 25 personnel involved in building new homes and offices.
- Trained numerous junior operators on the proper use and maintenance of construction equipment.
- Attained a 100% safety record through strict adherence to standard operating procedures.

CONSTRUCTION
OPERATIONS

- Operated bulldozers, roadgraders, and other heavy equipment in building over 25 miles of runway in record time, under combat conditions.
- Used scrapers and other heavy machinery to remove ice and snow from runways.
- Operated winches, cranes, and hoists in constructing over 200 new homes.

INTERNATIONAL

- Fluent in Spanish.

WORK HISTORY

Construction Supervisor, 23rd Engineer Battalion, McChord AFB, WA, 2003-Present
Construction Equipment Operator, 110th Construction Battalion, Keesler AFB, MO, 1999-2002

EDUCATION & TRAINING

A.A., Construction, Washington Community College, Seattle, WA, 2003
Air Force certified apprenticeship program in Heavy Construction, 1999
Diploma, Homer High School, Homer, NY, 1998

SUSAN B. ALMANN

589 Brighton View
Croton, NY 10520

914.555.8977   almann@protypeltd.com

CAREER OBJECTIVE

Human Resources Executive and member of the senior leadership team using proven expertise in guiding the design and execution of performance-based HR initiatives that achieve business objectives.

Provided vision and counsel in steering organizations through accelerated growth as well as in turning around underperforming businesses in both union and non-union environments. Diverse background includes multinational corporations in healthcare and manufacturing industries.

Core Competencies

- Long-Range Planning
- Recruitment & Staffing
- Employee Relations
- Leadership Development
- Succession Planning
- Compensation Design
- Culture Change
- M&A Integration
- HR Policies & Procedures
- Expatriate Programs

PROFESSIONAL EXPERIENCE

MARCON MANUFACTURING COMPANY, Peekskill, NY
Director, Human Resources (1996–Present)

Challenge: Recruited to create HR infrastructure to support business growth at a $30 million global manufacturing company with underachieving sales, exceedingly high turnover, and lack of cohesive management processes among business entities in U.S. and Asia.

Actions: Partnered with the President and Board of Directors to reorganize company, reduce overhead expenses, rebuild sales, and institute solid management infrastructure.

Results:
- Established HR with staff of 5, including development of policies and procedures; renegotiated cost-effective benefit programs that saved company $1.5 million annually.
- Reorganized operations and facilitated seamless integration of 150 employees from 2 new acquisitions within parent company.
- Reduced sales force turnover to nearly nonexistent, upgraded quality of candidates hired by implementing interview skills training and management development programs. Results led to improved sales performance.
- Recruited all management personnel; developed HR policies, procedures, and plans; and fostered team culture at newly built Malaysian plant with 125 employees.
- Initiated business reorganization plan, resulting in consolidation of New York and Virginia operations and $6.5 million in cost reductions.

BINGHAMTON COMPANY, New York, NY
Director, Human Resources & Administration (1993–1996)

Challenge: Lead HR and Administration function supporting 1,600 employees at $500 million manufacturer of medical equipment. Support company's turnaround efforts, business unit consolidations. and transition to consumer products focus.

Actions: Established cross-functional teams from each site and provided training in team building to coordinate product development efforts, implement new manufacturing processes, and speed products to market. Identified cost reduction opportunities; instrumental in reorganization initiatives that included closing union plant in Texas and building new plant in North Carolina. Managed HR staff of 12.

SUSAN B. ALMANN • Page 2

Director, Human Resources & Administration continued...

Results:
+ Instituted worldwide cross-functional team culture that provided the foundation for successful new product launches and recapture of company's leading edge despite intense competition.
+ Led flawless integration of 2 operations into single, cohesive European business unit, resulting in profitable business turnaround.
+ Restructured and positioned HR organization in the German business unit as customer-focused partner to support European sales and marketing units.
+ Initiated major benefit cost reductions of $3 million in year one and $1 million annually while gaining employee acceptance through concerted education and communications efforts.

<u>ARCAMED CORPORATION</u>, New York, NY
Manager, Human Resources (1989–1993)

Challenge: HR support to corporate office and field units of an $800 million organization with 150 global operations employing 4,500 people.

Actions: Promoted from Assistant Manager to lead staff of 10 in all HR and labor relations functions. Established separate international recruitment function and designed staffing plan to accommodate rapid business growth. Negotiated cost-effective benefits contracts for union and non-union employees.

Results:
+ Oversaw successful UAW, Teamsters, and labor contract negotiations.
+ Established and staffed HR function for major contract award with U.S. government agency.
+ Introduced incentive plans for field unit managers and an expatriate program that attracted both internal and external candidates for international assignments in the Middle East.
+ Managed HR issues associated with 2 business acquisitions while accomplishing a smooth transition and retention of all key personnel.
+ Restructured HR function with no service disruption to the business while saving $500,000 annually.

EDUCATION / AFFILIATIONS

M.B.A., Cornell University, New York, NY
B.A., Business Administration, Amherst College, Amherst, MA

Society for Human Resource Management
Human Resource Council of Albany

June Ellen Berringer
135 Killdeer Road, Apt. 721, Ewing, NJ 08628
(609) 771-7665 Residence Phone / Fax ▪ juneberringer21@yahoo.com

Medical Billing / Medical Records Technician

Dedicated, experienced professional with recent training in medical billing, medical terminology, and ICD-9-CM coding. Strong organizational, communications, and project management skills. Calm demeanor under stress; cooperative team leader. Proven multi-tasking / operations support skills. Adept in:

☑ Client Relationship Management   ☑ Medical Records Terminology   ☑ Budget Controls
☑ Customer Needs Management   ☑ Administrative Support   ☑ Project Coordination

KEY SUPPORTING SKILLS

▪ **Administration:** Diverse administrative expertise includes directing nationwide CHART (California Hospital Association Review Team) Program for American Hospital Association, managing seven-county sales territory in south central California, and maintaining large, upscale apartment complexes.

▪ **Time Management:** Demonstrate top-notch organizational skills, with ability to prioritize and multi-task. Developed records management systems to expedite back-office operations for sales generation, residential and retail property management, and meeting and event planning.

▪ **Communications:** Employ proactive problem-solving communications skills to generate "win-win" scenarios. Effectively communicated special situations and potential problem areas to management.

▪ **Personal Strengths:** Conscientious in following through on commitments and deadlines. Mature, discreet team player with experience interfacing with high-level executives and corporate clients.

EDUCATION
Medical Records Technician Program, The College of New Jersey, Ewing, NJ – 2005
Courses: Medical Terminology, Advanced Medical Terminology, Medical Billing, ICD-9-CM Coding
Associate of Arts Degree, San Diego Community College, San Diego, CA

PROFESSIONAL EXPERIENCE

Estate and Health Care Management, Princeton, NJ   2003 – 2005
✓ **Administrative Management.** Acted as prime interface with 60+ physicians, nurses, hospice, attorneys, CPA, stockbroker and insurance companies for elderly parents with progressive, debilitating illnesses. Managed health care appointments and treatment, as well as daily living arrangements onsite.

✓ **Records Management.** Submitted insurance claims and tracked insurance reimbursements. Oversaw distribution of $1 million estate. Arranged sale of house and distribution of all household goods.

Manufacturer's Representative   2001 – 2003
Pacific Printing, San Diego, CA and Elegant Communications, Inc., San Francisco, CA
Independent contractor representing fine gift, paper/stationary, and greeting card lines for two businesses.

✓ **Account Management.** Grew accounts by 45% (from 175 to 250) and increased sales by 20% in seven-county south central California territory. Generated 25 new key accounts (such as Yellowstone Park gift shops) through thorough market research, competitive market analysis and persuasive prospect interaction. Provided personalized customer service that generated 100% customer retention.

✓ **Customer Relationship Management.** Developed strong client communications networks, building relationships with 250 buyers for retail stores, museums, hospital gift shops, and nurseries. Educated buyers in 60+ lines of merchandise, updating them on retail trends and demographics-driven marketing.

June Ellen Berringer

(609) 771-7665 Residence Phone / Fax ▪ juneberringer21@yahoo.com   Page 2

PROFESSIONAL EXPERIENCE (continued)

Residential Property Management   1999 – 2001
Excelsior Properties, San Raphael, CA (1999-2000), and Seaside Views, San Diego, CA (2001)

✓ **Administrative Management.** Managed two upscale apartment communities (up to 516 units), with monthly rent collections of $432,000. Supervised on-site leasing, as well as 18 maintenance and grounds staff. Closely controlled $2,500 per month expense budget, monitoring five vendor services. Oversaw renovation of 35 apartment units, coordinating workflow and scheduling of carpet, flooring, paint, and fixture vendors with tenants.

✓ **Customer Service.** Maintained 92% residency rate and achieved 98% on-time rent collection by developing proactive tenant relationships programs. Initiated educational newsletter for tenants, as well as open-door policy for tenant complaints. Credited with stabilizing the tenant community through lawful evictions of known drug dealers.

Retail Property Management   1994 – 1999
Townsend Group Companies, San Diego and San Francisco, CA

✓ **Administrative Management.** Initiated and developed specialty leasing programs for three major developers (12 regional shopping centers) in high-profile metropolitan areas. Maintained high occupancy rates (95%) by actively recruiting retailers for year-round common area, as well as developing long-term, favorable leases for in-line sales operations.

✓ **Program Management.** Conceptualized and supervised design projects for kiosks and store décor, as well as for marketing communications (brochures, print advertising, and directories). Developed and met program budgets, generating in excess of $500,000 for each shopping center annually.

Meeting and Event Management   1993 – 1994
California Hospital Association, San Diego, CA

✓ **Program Management.** Served as Director of CHART (California Hospital Association Review Team) Program. Traveled statewide conducting peer review meetings for 8 to 10 state hospitals. Wrote reports based on participant feedback and critical observations and analysis of policies and procedures. Recommended policy and methodology changes, 90% of which were implemented by the Boards of the state hospitals.

✓ **Customer Service.** Facilitated in-house discussions on-site of hospital personnel and management at all levels to increase quality assurance, strengthen employee relations, improve customer service, and streamline processes and procedures. Initiated and encouraged constructive dialogues among groups that had a history of communication breakdowns.

COMPUTER SKILLS

☑ Training in Medical Billing software, Medical Records databases, and ICD-9-CM coding.
☑ Experienced in composing and editing letters, memos, marketing communications and reports.
☑ Utilize Windows XP, MS Office 2003 – Word, Excel, PowerPoint, Access, Internet Explorer, email.

SHEREN HENDERSEN

22 Dakota Street
Wellington, WA 98333-2222
(333) 444-4444
e-mail: Sheren@email.net

HOUSEKEEPER

"...an absolute model of calm efficiency, adaptability, general competence...." LB, Honokaa, HI

"... remarkable job managing an extremely high-pressure job with a limited budget and staff...quite conscientious and demonstrates personal pride in her work...a self-starter...very good at dealing with conflicting demands of the job...." —JJ, Operations Manager, Bay Resort

PROFILE

Professional housekeeper with adventurous, adaptable nature, and established reputation for reliability, follow-through, and commitment to service. Hands-on management style with proven ability to delegate, organize, and direct the work of others. Creative and innovative problem-solver, exercises good judgment and decision-making, keeps a clear head in times of crises. Easily establishes rapport and productive working relationships with co-workers and guests. Traveled extensively throughout United States.

AREAS OF EXPERTISE

- Housekeeping—cleaning procedures for hotels, motels, lodges, private homes, medical offices.
- Supervision—interview, hire, organize, schedule, train, and evaluate staff.
- Emergencies—trained in procedures to follow in case of fire, flood, broken pipes, etc.— CPR/First Aid Certification
- Inventory—stocking, ordering of linens and cleaning supplies.
- Budget—evaluation and compliance.

SUMMARY OF EXPERIENCE

Executive Housekeeper, Bay Village, Inc., Okay, Washington   1995–present

Oversee daily cleaning and maintenance of 38 cabins, 4 public areas including restrooms and shower houses, and guest kitchen.

Interview, hire, train, schedule, and supervise housekeeping staff. Inspect all cabins and public areas twice daily—before and after cleaning. Wash, dry, fold, and restock, provide hot-tub towels—bundle for delivery to outside laundry. Order cleaning supplies.

Evaluate departmental monthly budget for scheduling and wages—operate consistently within budget.

Assistant Manager, Hoot Owl Lodge, Gato, AK   winter 1994–95

Oversaw housekeeping for busy, well-attended, lodge in remote area of Alaska—consisted of log cabin with bar, restaurant, game area, and six cabins. Occasionally tended bar and cooked meals. Stocked inventory when supplies were delivered. Drove snowmobile.

Executive Housekeeper, Bellingham Travel Lodge, Wellington, WA   1992–1993

Over daily assignments, cleaning, inspection, and laundry for 115 rooms. Substituted for front desk clerk.

Housekeeper, by contract   1989–1990
Wellington News Building and Electric Power Building

EDUCATION

Valley College—Business Machines
Wellington County Vocation School—Word Processing / Secretarial

Appendix C

Job Search Letter Examples

THE FOLLOWING LETTERS represent only a few of the many types of letters used in effective job search campaigns (see Tip #161):

- Resume letters
- Cover letters
- "T" letters
- Approach letters
- Thank-you letters

Some of these letters, such as the resume letter on page 208 and the "T" letter on page 210, can substitute for resumes.

Each of these letters follows the many letter writing tips outlined in Chapter 8. Pay particular attention to the proactive tone of the letters. Most of the letters include some sort of action statement that sets the stage for following up with a telephone call.

Additional examples of effective job search letters, including several unusual letters, can be found in our three companion volumes: *201 Dynamite Job Search Letters*, *Nail the Cover Letter!*, and *High Impact Resumes and Letters* (Impact Publications).

Resume Letter

4921 Tyler Drive
Washington, D.C. 20011
March 15, 20 ____

Doris Stevens
STR Corporation
179 South Trail
Rockville, Maryland 21101

Dear Ms. Stevens:

STR Corporation is one of the most dynamic computer companies in the nation. In addition to being a leader in the field of small business computers, STR has a progressive employee training and development program which could very well become a model for other organizations. This is the type of organization I am interested in joining.

I am seeking a training position with a computer firm which would utilize my administrative, communication, and planning abilities to develop effective training and counseling programs. My experience includes:

<u>Administration</u>: Supervised instructors and counselors. Coordinated job vacancy and training information for businesses, industries, and schools.

<u>Communication</u>: Conducted over 100 workshops on interpersonal skills, stress management, and career planning. Frequent guest speaker to various agencies and private firms. Experienced writer of training manuals and public relations materials.

<u>Planning</u>: Planned and developed counseling programs for 5,000 employees. Reorganized interviewing and screening processes for public employment agency. Developed program of individualized and group counseling for community school.

In addition, I am completing my Ph.D. in industrial psychology with emphasis on developing training and counseling programs for technical personnel.

Could we meet to discuss your program as well as how my experience might relate to your needs? I will call your office on Tuesday morning, March 23, to arrange a convenient time to meet with you.

I especially want to show you a model employee counseling and career development program I recently developed. Perhaps you may find it useful for your work with STR.

Sincerely yours,

James C. Astor

James C. Astor
astorc@mymail.com

Cover Letter

2842 South Plaza
Chicago, Illinois 60228
March 12, 20 ___

David C. Johnson
Director of Personnel
Bank of Chicago
490 Michigan Avenue
Chicago, Illinois 60222

Dear Mr. Johnson:

The accompanying resume is in response to your listing in the Chicago Tribune for a loan officer.

I am especially interested in this position because my experience with the Small Business Administration has prepared me for understanding the financial needs and problems of the business community from the perspectives of both lenders and borrowers. I wish to use this experience with a growing and community-conscious bank such as yours.

I would appreciate an opportunity to meet with you to discuss how my experience will best meet your needs. My ideas on how to improve small business financing may be of particular interest to you. Therefore, I will call your office on the morning of March 17 to inquire if a meeting can be scheduled at a convenient time.

I look forward to meeting you.

Sincerely yours,

Joyce Pitman

Joyce Pitman
pitmanj@mymail.com

"T" Letter: Responding to Classified Ad

16 Bella Vista Place
Cincinnati, OH 45206
April 16, 20___

Ms. Cecily Dorfmann
Vice President, Human Resources
Nair Industries
257 Vine Street
Cincinnati, OH 45202

Re: Sales Manager, Cincinnati Enquirer, April 12

Dear Ms. Dorfmann:

As a Sales Manager, I have planned and scheduled direct sales programs and trade shows with consistently profitable results. Here is a list of my qualifications as they relate to your requirements for the position of Sales Manager:

Your Requirements	My Qualifications
2 years Direct Sales Management (Self-contained sales region)	Over 7 years aggressive direct sales management experience as proven by opening 8 area offices which escalated regional sales average to #1 position among 200 offices.
Individual Sales Experience	Dynamic individual sales success proved by exceeding all sales goals for 18 months and reaching "Top ½%" among 250.
Excellent Verbal and Written	Exceptional Communicator as demonstrated by over 40 major group presentations, writing "direct sales" promotional materials and column (reaching 11,000) and 3-day demonstrations at 22 national trade shows.
Problem Solving and Strategic Planning Skills	Excellent Problem Solver and Strategic Planner indicated by structuring daily control meetings for staff of 25 resolving problem of "peak time" business loss (increased 35%)
Marketing and Corporate Office	Strong Marketing Experience (4 years) at corporate office level, proven skills in creating innovative team format and realigning 35 inside-outside sales/support staff to generate 15% sales increase to $3.5MM.

Enclosed is a resume that lists other accomplishments that may be of interest to you.

I look forward to meeting with you to explore the use of my talents to support the growth of your company. I will call on Wednesday, April 21, to schedule an interview at your convenience.

Sincerely,

Susan Ariani

Susan Ariani
Enclosure

Approach Letter
Referral

821 Stevens Point
Boston, MA 01990
April 14, 20 ____

Terri Fulton
Director of Personnel
TRS Corporation
6311 W. Dover
Boston, MA 01991

Dear Ms. Fulton:

Alice O'Brien suggested that I contact you about my interest in personnel management. She said you are one of the best people to talk to in regard to careers in personnel.

I am leaving government after seven years of increasingly responsible experience in personnel. I am especially interested in working with a large private firm. However, before I venture further into the job market, I want to benefit from the experience and knowledge of others in the field who might advise me on opportunities for someone with my qualifications.

Perhaps we could meet briefly sometime during the next two weeks to discuss my career plans. I have several questions which I believe you could help clarify. I will call your office on Tuesday, April 22, to schedule a meeting time.

I look forward to discussing my plans with you.

Sincerely yours,

Katherine Kelly

Katherine Kelly
kellyk@mymail.com

Approach Letter
Cold Turkey

2189 West Church Street
New York, NY 10011
May 3, 20 _____

Patricia Dotson, Director
Northeast Association for
  the Elderly
9930 Jefferson Street
New York, NY 10013

Dear Ms. Dotson:

I have been impressed with your work with the elderly. Your organization takes a community perspective in trying to integrate the concerns of the elderly with those of other community groups. Perhaps other organizations will soon follow your lead.

I am anxious to meet you and learn more about your work. My background with the city Volunteer Services Program involved frequent contacts with elderly volunteers. From this experience I decided I preferred working primarily with the elderly.

However, before I pursue my interest further, I need to talk to people with experience in gerontology. In particular, I would like to know more about careers with the elderly as well as how my background might best be used in the field of gerontology.

I am hoping you can assist me in this matter. I would like to meet with you briefly to discuss several of my concerns. I will call next week to see if your schedule permits such a meeting.

I look forward to meeting you.

Sincerely,

Carol Timms

Carol Timms
timmsc@mymail.com

Thank-You Letter
Post-Informational Interview

9910 Thompson Drive
Cleveland, Ohio 43382
June 21, 20 _____

Jane Evans, Director
Evans Finance Corporation
2122 Forman Street
Cleveland, Ohio 43380

Dear Ms. Evans:

Your advice was most helpful in clarifying my questions on careers in finance. I am now reworking my resume and have included many of your thoughtful suggestions. I will send you a copy next week.

Thanks so much for taking time from your busy schedule to see me. I will keep in contact and follow through on your suggestion to see Sarah Cook about opportunities with the Cleveland-Akron Finance Company.

Sincerely,

Daryl Haines

Daryl Haines
hainesd@mymail.com

Thank-You Letter
Post-Job Interview

2962 Forrest Drive
Denver, Colorado 82171
May 28, 20 ____

Thomas F. Harris
Director, Personnel Department
Coastal Products Incorporated
7229 Lakewood Drive
Denver, Colorado 82170

Dear Mr. Harris:

Thank you again for the opportunity to interview for the marketing position. I appreciated your hospitality and enjoyed meeting you and members of your staff.

The interview convinced me of how compatible my background, interest, and skills are with the goals of Coastal Products Incorporated. My prior marketing experience with the Department of Commerce has prepared me to take a major role in developing both domestic and international marketing strategies. I am confident my work for you will result in increased profits within the first two years.

For more information on the new product promotion program I mentioned, call David Garrett at the Department of Commerce; his number is 202/726-0132. I talked to Dave this morning and mentioned your interest in this program.

I look forward to meeting you again.

Sincerely,

Tim Potter

Tim Potter
pottert@mymail.com

Thank-You Letter
Job Rejection

564 Court Street
St. Louis, MO 53167
April 29, 20 ____

Ralph Ullman, President
S.T. Ayer Corporation
6921 Southern Blvd.
St. Louis, MO 53163

Dear Mr. Ullman:

I appreciated your consideration for the Research Associate position. While I am disappointed in not being selected, I learned a great deal about your corporation, and I enjoyed meeting with you and your staff. I felt particularly good about the professional manner in which you conducted the interview.

Please keep me in mind for future consideration. I have a strong interest in your company. I believe we would work well together. I will be closely following the progress of your company over the coming months. Perhaps we will be in touch with each other at some later date.

Best wishes.

Sincerely,

Martin Tollins

Martin Tollins
tollinsm@mymail.com

Thank-You Letter
Job Offer Acceptance

7694 James Court
San Francisco, CA 94826
June 7, 20 _____

Judith Greene
Vice President
West Coast Airlines
2400 Van Ness
San Francisco, CA 94829

Dear Ms. Greene:

I am pleased to accept your offer, and I am looking forward to joining you and your staff next month.

The customer relations position is ideally suited to my background and interests. I assure you I will give you my best effort in making this an effective position within your company.

I understand I will begin work on July. If, in the meantime, I need to complete any paper work or take care of any other matters, please contact me.

I enjoyed meeting with you and your staff and appreciated the professional manner in which the hiring was conducted.

Sincerely,

Joan Kitner

Joan Kitner
kitnerj@mymail.com

Index

The Authors

FOR MORE THAN TWO DECADES Ron and Caryl Krannich have pursued a passion – assisting hundreds of thousands of individuals, from students, the unemployed, and ex-offenders to military personnel, international job seekers, and CEOs, in making critical job and career transitions. Focusing on key job search skills, career changes, and employment fields, their impressive body of work has helped shape career thinking and behavior both in the United States and abroad. Their sound advice has changed numerous lives, including their own!

Ron and Caryl are two of America's leading career and travel writers who have authored more than 80 books. A former Peace Corps Volunteer and Fulbright Scholar, Ron received his Ph.D. in Political Science from Northern Illinois University. Caryl received her Ph.D. in Speech Communication from Penn State University. Together they operate Development Concepts Incorporated, a training, consulting, and publishing firm in Virginia.

The Krannichs are former university professors, high school teachers, management trainers, and consultants. As trainers and consultants, they have completed numerous projects on management, career development, local government, population planning, and rural development in the United States and abroad. Their career books focus on key job search skills, military and civilian career transitions, government and international careers, travel jobs, and nonprofit organizations and include such

221

classics as *High Impact Resumes and Letters, Interview for Success,* and *Change Your Job, Change Your Life.*

Their books represent one of today's most comprehensive collections of career writing. With over 3 million copies in print, their publications are widely available in bookstores, libraries, and career centers. No strangers to the world of Internet employment and travel, they have written *America's Top Internet Job Sites, Haldane's Best Employment Websites for Professionals, The Directory of Websites for International Jobs,* and *Travel Planning on the Internet* and published several Internet recruitment and job search books. Ron served as the first Work Abroad Advisor to Monster.com. Ron and Caryl also have developed several career-related websites: www.impactpublications.com, www.winningthejob.com, www.exoffenderreentry.com, and www.veterans world.com. Many of their career tips appear on such major websites as www.monster.com, www.careerbuilder.com, www.campuscareercenter. com, and www.employmentguide.com.

Ron and Caryl live a double life with travel being their best kept *"do what you love"* career secret. Authors of more than 20 travel-shopping guidebooks on various destinations around the world, they continue to pursue their international and travel interests through their innovative *Treasures and Pleasures of . . . Best of the Best* travel-shopping series and related websites: www.ishoparoundtheworld.com and www.travel-smarter.com. When not found at their home and business in Virginia, they are probably somewhere in Europe, Asia, Africa, the Middle East, the South Pacific, the Caribbean, or the Americas following their other passion – researching and writing about quality antiques, arts, crafts, jewelry, hotels, restaurants, and sightseeing as well as adhering to the career advice they give to others: *"Pursue a passion that enables you to do what you really love to do."* Their passion is best represented on www.ishoparound theworld.com.

As both career and travel experts, the Krannichs' work is frequently featured in major newspapers, magazines, and newsletters as well as on radio, television, and the Internet. Available for interviews, consultation, and presentations, they can be contacted as follows:

Ron and Caryl Krannich
krannich@impactpublications.com

Career Resources

THE FOLLOWING CAREER RESOURCES are available directly from Impact Publications. Full descriptions of each title, as well as several downloadable catalogs and specialty flyers, can be found at www.impactpublications.com. Complete the following form or list the titles, include shipping (see formula at the end), enclose payment, and send your order to:

IMPACT PUBLICATIONS
9104 Manassas Drive, Suite N
Manassas Park, VA 20111-5211 USA
1-800-361-1055 (orders only)
Tel. 703-361-7300 or Fax 703-335-9486
Email address: query@impactpublications.com
Quick & easy online ordering: www.impactpublications.com

Orders from individuals must be prepaid by check, money order, or major credit card. We accept telephone, fax, and email orders.

Qty.	TITLES	Price	TOTAL
	Other Titles By Authors		
____	201 Dynamite Job Search Letters	$19.95	____
____	The $100,000+ Entrepreneur	$19.95	____
____	America's Top Internet Job Sites	$19.95	____
____	America's Top 100 Jobs for People Without a Four-Year Degree	$19.95	____
____	America's Top Jobs for People Re-Entering the Workforce	$19.95	____
____	Best Jobs for the 21st Century	$19.95	____
____	Best Resumes and CVs for International Jobs	$24.95	____
____	Best Resumes and Letters for Ex-Offenders	$19.95	____
____	Blue Collar Resume and Job Hunting Guide	$15.95	____
____	Change Your Job, Change Your Life	$21.95	____
____	Complete Guide to Public Employment	$19.95	____
____	Directory of Websites for International Jobs	$19.95	____
____	Discover the Best Jobs for You	$15.95	____

_____ Dynamite Salary Negotiations	$15.95	_____
_____ The Ex-Offender's Job Hunting Guide	$17.95	_____
_____ The Ex-Offender's Quick Job Hunting Guide	$9.95	_____
_____ Get a Raise in 7 Days	$14.95	_____
_____ Haldane's Best Answers to Tough Interview Questions	$15.95	_____
_____ Haldane's Best Cover Letters for Professionals	$15.95	_____
_____ Haldane's Best Resumes for Professionals	$15.95	_____
_____ High Impact Resumes and Letters	$19.95	_____
_____ I Can't Believe They Asked Me That!	$17.95	_____
_____ I Want to Do Something Else, But I'm Not Sure What It Is	$15.95	_____
_____ Interview for Success	$15.95	_____
_____ The Job Hunting Guide: Transitioning From College to Career	$14.95	_____
_____ Job Hunting Tips for People With Hot and Not-So-Hot Backgrounds	$17.95	_____
_____ Job Interview Tips for People With Not-So-Hot Backgrounds	$14.95	_____
_____ Jobs for Travel Lovers	$19.95	_____
_____ Military Resumes and Cover Letters	$21.95	_____
_____ Military Transition to Civilian Success	$21.95	_____
_____ Nail the Cover Letter!	$17.95	_____
_____ Nail the Job Interview!	$13.95	_____
_____ Nail the Resume!	$17.95	_____
_____ No One Will Hire Me!	$13.95	_____
_____ Overcoming Barriers to Employment	$17.95	_____
_____ Resume, Application, and Letter Tips for People With Hot and Not-So-Hot Backgrounds	$17.95	_____
_____ Salary Negotiation Tips for Professionals	$16.95	_____
_____ Savvy Interviewing: The Nonverbal Advantage	$10.95	_____
_____ The Savvy Networker	$13.95	_____
_____ The Savvy Resume Writer	$12.95	_____
_____ Win the Interview, Win the Job	$15.95	_____

Resumes, Letters, and Portfolios

_____ 101 Great Tips for a Dynamite Resume	$13.95	_____
_____ 175 Best Cover Letters	$14.95	_____
_____ Best KeyWords for Resumes, Cover Letters, & Interviews	$17.95	_____
_____ Best Career Transition Resumes for $100,000+ Jobs	$24.95	_____
_____ Best Resumes for $75,000+ Executive Jobs	$16.95	_____
_____ Best Resumes for $100,000+ Jobs	$24.95	_____
_____ Best Resumes for People Without a Four-Year Degree	$19.95	_____
_____ Best Cover Letters for $100,000+ Jobs	$24.95	_____
_____ Blue Collar Resumes	$11.99	_____
_____ College Grad Resumes to Land $75,000+ Jobs	$24.95	_____
_____ Competency-Based Resumes	$13.99	_____
_____ Cover Letters for Dummies	$16.99	_____
_____ Cover Letters That Knock 'Em Dead	$12.95	_____
_____ Create Your Own Digital Portfolio	$19.95	_____
_____ e-Resumes	$16.95	_____
_____ Executive Job Search for $100,000 to $1 Million+ Jobs	$24.95	_____
_____ Expert Resumes for People Returning to Work	$16.95	_____
_____ Gallery of Best Cover Letters	$18.95	_____
_____ Gallery of Best Resumes	$18.95	_____
_____ Resume Shortcuts	$14.95	_____
_____ Resumes for Dummies	$16.99	_____
_____ Resumes That Knock 'Em Dead	$12.95	_____
_____ Winning Letters That Overcome Barriers to Employment	$17.95	_____
_____ World's Greatest Resumes	$14.95	_____

Testing and Assessment

_____ Aptitude, Personality, and Motivation Tests	$17.95	_____
_____ Career Tests	$12.95	_____

_____ Discover What You're Best At $14.00 _____
_____ Do What You Are $18.95 _____
_____ I Could Do Anything If Only I Knew What It Was $16.00 _____
_____ I Don't Know What I Want, But I Know It's Not This $14.00 _____
_____ I Want to Do Something Else, But I'm Not Sure What It Is $15.95 _____
_____ I'm Not Crazy, I'm Just Not You $16.95 _____
_____ Now, Discover Your Strengths $30.00 _____
_____ The Pathfinder $16.00 _____
_____ What Should I Do With My Life? $14.95 _____
_____ What Type Am I? $14.95 _____
_____ What's Your Type of Career? $18.95 _____

Attitude and Motivation

_____ 100 Ways to Motivate Yourself $14.99 _____
_____ Attitude Is Everything $14.95 _____
_____ Change Your Attitude $15.99 _____
_____ Reinventing Yourself $18.99 _____

Inspiration and Empowerment

_____ 7 Habits of Highly Effective People (2nd Edition) $15.00 _____
_____ The 8th Habit: From Effectiveness to Greatness $26.00 _____
_____ 101 Secrets of Highly Effective Speakers $15.95 _____
_____ Awaken the Giant Within $16.00 _____
_____ Change Your Thinking, Change Your Life $24.95 _____
_____ Dream It Do It $16.95 _____
_____ Finding Your Own North Star $14.95 _____
_____ Goals! $15.95 _____
_____ It's Only Too Late If You Don't Start Now $15.00 _____
_____ Life Strategies $13.95 _____
_____ Magic of Thinking Big $13.00 _____
_____ Power of Positive Thinking $12.95 _____
_____ Purpose-Driven Life $19.99 _____
_____ Self Matters $14.00 _____
_____ Ten Commandments to Your Success $11.95 _____
_____ Who Moved My Cheese? $19.95 _____

Career Exploration and Job Strategies

_____ 5 Patterns of Extraordinary Careers $17.95 _____
_____ 25 Jobs That Have It All $12.95 _____
_____ 50 Best Jobs for Your Personality $16.95 _____
_____ 50 Cutting Edge Jobs $15.95 _____
_____ 95 Mistakes Job Seekers Make & How to Avoid Them $13.95 _____
_____ 100 Great Jobs and How to Get Them $17.95 _____
_____ 101 Ways to Recession-Proof Your Career $14.95 _____
_____ 200 Best Jobs for College Grads $16.95 _____
_____ 250 Best Jobs Through Apprenticeships $24.95 _____
_____ 300 Best Jobs Without a Four-Year Degree $16.95 _____
_____ America's Top 100 Jobs for People Without a Four-Year Degree $19.95 _____
_____ Best Entry-Level Jobs $16.95 _____
_____ Best Jobs for the 21st Century $19.95 _____
_____ Career Change $14.95 _____
_____ Cool Careers for Dummies $19.99 _____
_____ Directory of Executive Recruiters $49.95 _____
_____ Five Secrets to Finding a Job $12.95 _____
_____ A Fork in the Road: A Career Planning Guide for Young Adults $14.95 _____
_____ Great Careers in Two Years $19.95 _____
_____ High-Tech Careers for Low-Tech People $14.95 _____
_____ How to Get a Job and Keep It $16.95 _____
_____ How to Get Interviews From Classified Job Ads $14.95 _____

____	How to Succeed Without a Career Path	$13.95 ____
____	Job Search Handbook for People With Disabilities	$17.95 ____
____	Knock 'Em Dead	$14.95 ____
____	Me, Myself, and I, Inc.	$17.95 ____
____	Monster Careers	$18.00 ____
____	Quick Prep Careers	$18.95 ____
____	Quit Your Job and Grow Some Hair	$15.95 ____
____	Rites of Passage at $100,000 to $1 Million+	$29.95 ____
____	Suddenly Unemployed	$14.95 ____
____	Top 100 Health-Care Careers	$24.95 ____
____	What Color Is Your Parachute?	$17.95 ____

Career Directories

____	Associations USA	$75.00 ____
____	Enhanced Occupational Outlook Handbook	$39.95 ____
____	Job Hunter's Sourcebook	$160.00 ____
____	Occupational Outlook Handbook	$17.95 ____
____	O*NET Dictionary of Occupational Titles	$39.95 ____
____	Professional Careers Sourcebook	$150.00 ____
____	Vocational Careers Sourcebook	$150.00 ____

Internet Job Search

____	100 Top Internet Job Sites	$12.95 ____
____	America's Top Internet Job Sites	$19.95 ____
____	Career Exploration On the Internet	$24.95 ____
____	Guide to Internet Job Searching	$14.95 ____
____	Job Hunting on the Internet	$11.95 ____
____	Job Seeker's Online Goldmine	$13.95 ____

Networking

____	A Foot in the Door	$14.95 ____
____	How to Work a Room	$14.00 ____
____	Masters of Networking	$16.95 ____
____	Networking for Job Search and Career Success	$16.95 ____

Dress, Image, and Etiquette

____	Dressing Smart for Men	$16.95 ____
____	Dressing Smart for Women	$16.95 ____
____	Power Etiquette	$14.95 ____

Interviews

____	101 Dynamite Questions to Ask At Your Job Interview	$13.95 ____
____	Job Interviews for Dummies	$16.99 ____
____	KeyWords to Nail Your Job Interview	$17.95 ____
____	Sweaty Palms	$13.95 ____

Salary Negotiations

____	Dynamite Salary Negotiations	$15.95 ____
____	Get a Raise in 7 Days	$14.95 ____
____	Salary Negotiation Tips for Professionals	$16.95 ____

Ex-Offenders in Transition

____	9 to 5 Beats Ten to Life	$15.00 ____
____	99 Days and a Get Up	$9.95 ____
____	Best Resumes and Letters for Ex-Offenders	$19.95 ____

_____	Ex-Offender's Quick Job Hunting Guide	$9.95	_____
_____	Man, I Need a Job	$7.95	_____
_____	Putting the Bars Behind You (6 books)	$57.95	_____

Government Jobs

_____	Book of U.S. Government Jobs	$21.95	_____
_____	FBI Careers	$19.95	_____
_____	Post Office Jobs	$19.95	_____
_____	Ten Steps to a Federal Job	$39.95	_____

International and Travel Jobs

_____	Back Door Guide to Short-Term Job Adventures	$21.95	_____
_____	Careers in International Affairs	$24.95	_____
_____	Directory of Websites for International Jobs	$19.95	_____
_____	International Job Finder	$19.95	_____
_____	Jobs for Travel Lovers	$19.95	_____
_____	Teaching English Abroad	$15.95	_____

SUBTOTAL _____

Virginia residents add 5% sales tax _____

POSTAGE/HANDLING ($5 for first
product and 8% of SUBTOTAL) $5.00

8% of SUBTOTAL -- _____

TOTAL ENCLOSED ------------------------- _____

SHIP TO:

NAME _____

ADDRESS: _____

_____

_____

PAYMENT METHOD:

❏ I enclose check/money order for $ _____ made payable to
IMPACT PUBLICATIONS.

❏ Please charge $ _____ to my credit card:
❏ Visa ❏ MasterCard ❏ American Express ❏ Discover

Card # _____ Expiration date: ____ / ____

Signature _____

Keep in Touch...
On the Web!

7-12-06

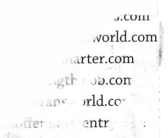

....com

...world.com

...arter.com

...ngth..ob.com

...rans..world.co

...offer....entry...

201 DYNAMITE JOB SEARCH LETTERS